ENDORSEMENTS

In *Walking Through Walls* Brad Larson frames the integration of faith and work in a compelling and practical narrative that is sure to challenge you.

—Ken Coleman, Author of *One Question:
Life-Changing Answers from Today's Leading Voices*

Walking Through Walls is an insightful book that connects work as a gift from God that leads to joy, purpose, and significance. Brad Larson does a great job showing we don't have to work for the weekend. Instead, we are invited to work for God's glory.

—Scott Brooks, Lead Pastor of
The Door Church in Coppell, TX

Brad Larson does an incredible job of applying his biblical wisdom and the Word of God to everyday experiences in your job that will help you stay focused on doing work that matters.

—Nick Stavinoha, Baseball Agent and Former Major
League Baseball Player

A biblically-driven book that displays practical advice of how to integrate faith and work as one, and take them both back into a newly-discovered missional environment of the everyday.

—Aaron Fair, President of Known as The Way,
and Acts 29 Church Planter in the
Southeast Asia Emerging Regions

The notion that we can utilize our jobs or careers to create a more intimate relationship with Jesus, not just to support ourselves financially, is powerful—thrilled to see Brad bring this conversation to light.

—Willie Morris, Founder & CEO, Faithbox

In *Walking Through Walls*, Brad Larson reminds us of our spiritual purpose to ultimately glorify God. Larson does an amazing job of providing tangible ways to transform your career and the workplace through the power of the Holy Spirit.

—Brittany Merrill Underwood,
Founder & President, Akola Project

WALKING THROUGH WALLS

Connecting Faith and Work

BRAD LARSON

LUCIDBOOKS

Walking Through Walls

All scripture quotations, unless otherwise indicated, are taken from the
Holy Bible, English Standard Version (ESV).

First Printing 2015

ISBN 10: 1-63296-066-4
ISBN 13: 978-1-63296-066-5
eISBN 10: 1-63296-067-2
eISBN 13: 978-1-63296-067-2

Special Sales: Most Lucid Books titles are available in special quantity
discounts. Custom imprinting or excerpting can also be done to fit
special needs. Contact Lucid Books at info@lucidbooks.net.

DEDICATION

To Lindsay, Liam, and Lila—my treasure and my heart.

TABLE OF CONTENTS

ACKNOWLEDGEMENTS

Oh man, where to start. Thank you to Lindsay, Liam, and Lila for being my rock and my safe place. (And thanks to Lindsay for never letting me take this too seriously.) To Dad, who taught me to work and to serve others. You live the Golden Rule. You are my hero and my inspiration. To Mom, for always believing in me and for encouraging me to dance. You see the potential I don't, and you have made me unafraid to fail. To Casey, you have always had my back. I am so proud of the woman you've become. To Allie (Grallis), who beat everyone to the punch on the Kickstarter and was the first supporter! To Bob and Diana, my dear friends and my second set of parents. I cannot explain to you how much your love, support, and confidence mean to me in my various endeavors. To Brad Neathery, my partner-in-crime and constant encourager to think big and do big things. Our lunch at the Thai place really escalated things. To the Lucid Books team (Casey and Sammantha), you guys stood behind me and believed in this book. You are not only true professionals, but you are also fantastic coaches and loyal friends—and sometimes borderline therapists. To Scott Brooks, my pastor and dear brother in Christ. You took me under your wing, and your iron sharpened me and brought me closer to Jesus. To Bob, Keith, Christian, Steve, and Josh—my band of elder brothers. To all of the Kickstarter supporters, all 50 of you. You cannot understand what your support means to me. You made this book happen. To Elliott Hillock, your friendship lifted me, and your seed money for Joyfully Yoked shoved the effort forward. Everyone deserves to have a friend like you, but few ever do. To Kevin Rudolph, you shaped my faith at a very impressionable time and soaked my heart with an understanding of the grace of Christ.

Most importantly, I thank my Lord and savior Jesus Christ, who has taken my heart of stone and put into my chest a heart of flesh.

Last, to you, the reader of this book. Thanks for picking it up and reading it. Your time is valuable, so I pray that this investment of your life pays eternal dividends.

INTRODUCTION

Years ago I realized my Sundays were different from my Mondays. Going to work each day, I felt like I had Jesus in my pocket and I didn't know what to do with Him. I loved my job and had a vibrant faith, but I could not figure out how the two intersected.

I wasn't facing just an internal struggle in my mind. There were both internal and external factors that kept me from integrating my faith and my work—internal and external walls. The internal walls were built within me, upon wrong thinking, obliviousness, or weak faith. The external walls were built by someone else. And these walls were a problem. I realized that these barriers—these walls—stood between me and faith-filled work. I had faith in Christ and I had a great career, but due to these walls I had created a separation between the two. I wanted to figure out what was going on.

As I continued to explore the subject of faith and work as a regular working guy, my passion and angst for the subject grew. You might even say it festered. No one I knew talked about it, the pastors I listened to weren't talking about it, and the media certainly wasn't talking about it. It seemed the laymen like me were too busy at work to bring the topic to light.

So I decided to write.

Writing is a natural outlet for my brain and soul. It is something I can't *not do*. So writing about the connection between faith and work was natural. But how? Through what platform? Surely it wouldn't be helpful to write in isolation where no one else could join me on the journey. I figured a blog would work.

Now here is when my insecurities and cowardice welled up within me and told me to shut my mouth. At the time I was in the white collar world of corporate real estate, and my colleagues were busy doing deals, not exploring the meaning of their work. Senior vice presidents at commercial real estate companies should be working, not writing. I doubted whether or not I should pursue writing at all. My mind went crazy with doubt. *What would your colleagues think? This could alienate clients who aren't Christians. You will be pigeon-holed as the Bible-thumper.* I think it's quite possible there was some Ephesians 6 spiritual warfare going on here, but for the most part I think I was dealing with my cowardice.

I told my buddy Brad about the angst and how I wanted to write. I didn't mention the internal battle going on in my head. I just mentioned that I was thinking about starting a blog on the subject of faith and work. Brad is by nature an encourager and so he nudged me forward. As the owner of a branding agency, Brad even built me a website for the blog—and my excuses started to vanish. We called it "Joyfully Yoked," which meant as Christians we are meant to be joyfully yoked to our purpose of work.

So at this point you'd think I'd start writing, right? Yeah, you'd think. I shelved the blog for months. But God wasn't cool with that.

One morning after de-icing my truck's windshield, I headed to the office. It was an ordinary winter morning, maybe a Tuesday. As I neared the end of my neighborhood, I had one of those epiphany moments where God clearly presses something into the conscience that must be acted upon. God didn't speak audibly, but I knew exactly what He was calling me to do. I was going to write a book on the connection between faith and work. Now, understand I had not written even a word about this subject and I had a blog collecting dust in the corner and—a book? This is backwards. You are supposed to blog and build what people in the publishing business call a "platform" before writing a book. And here I was, too scared to write a blog post but feeling compelled to write a book.

God has such a great sense of humor.

As I drove along, the heater warming my legs, I figured I'd just grab a flash drive and get started. The proceeds of the book would go to my church to help fund its campaign to build a new building. *Yeah, that makes sense. Why not?*

I called my wife, Lindsay, and she was all for it. She said to go ahead, not knowing what she was getting herself into. Scott, the lead pastor of our church and my dear friend, encouraged me forward. And, again, my buddy Brad breathed wind into my sails. I had told too many people now—I could not hide. I was committed.

In today's noisy world, books do not sell themselves. There are warehouses full of well-written books rotting because no one knows that they exist. I learned this and realized I needed to fire up the blog if this book was going to sell. And it needed to sell, both to provide funds for the church and to change people's lives. As things took shape I realized that while the former is a worthy goal on its own, the latter is the better part of what God is up to.

Because no one in my personal network—save Lindsay, Scott, and Brad—knew what I was up to, I published a Facebook post letting my little world know what I was up to. Then I started fumbling through my first blog post. Then a second. Third. Fourth . . .

What has happened between that time and now is hard to explain. Not only has God taught me more than I can recall or comprehend, but I have had the pleasure of sitting down with

brilliant thinkers, media personalities, and business leaders
with an integrated spiritual and work life. It has been a wild
ride.

Having researched and learned about this topic over the
past several years, I realize the importance of integrating faith
in Christ and the work of our hands more than ever. As our
culture changes, so too does the workplace. And for those of
us who follow Jesus, it is imperative that we get our mind right
about the gift of work. This issue burns strong and hot in my
heart. And I am so grateful to God for pushing me outside of
my comfort zone to explore this important topic.

~

Before we get going, I want to clarify what I mean by work. You work. I work. Whatever our hands find to do on a daily basis is our work. Work does not have to mean business, though business is certainly included in the definition. A stay-at-home mom works, so do students. My hope is that an inclusive definition of work will help us all keep God's promises in view in our daily grind, whether we deliver papers or install toilets or chase bad guys. This book isn't just for business folk like me.

In Chapter 1, we will explore God's design for work. God made work to be good. Work existed before The Fall of man in Genesis 3, so we know that work was intended to be a blessing. Adam and Eve worked in The Garden and we can expect to work in heaven. But Genesis 3 tells us that the consequence of sin is that work is cursed and that we'll have to work our way through thorns and thistles. However, it is important to remember that those in Christ aren't cursed. Because of the sanctification process, followers of Christ are becoming more like Jesus every day, and our work follows our path of sanctification.

In Chapter 2, we will see what it looks like to integrate faith and work. What happens when the faith in your heart guides the work of your hands? You work faithfully, risk big, and share your faith. When your faith guides your work (versus fear, greed, etc.), you are free to work and explore with boldness.

In Chapter 3, we approach the first wall: your mindset on money. You see, money is morally neutral, but having an unhealthy focus on money becomes a wall for us spiritually. If you don't understand the financial reward for your work, you won't follow the right path while working. We will address the lie of the prosperity gospel and the poverty gospel, the two most common distortions of money that you just might hear from the pulpit or on the street.

In Chapter 4, we pull back the curtain on the wall of bad assumptions. You see, we carry accepted truths into our daily

lives, and we rely upon them without question. The sun will
rise. Air will fill our lungs. Work is meaningless. Wait—what?
Our culture and our experiences shape our assumptions.
Assumptions aren't themselves bad, but we need to put them on
trial to make sure they serve their purpose. In this chapter we'll
address some common faulty assumptions and then discuss a
corrective assumption for each to get us on the right track.

In Chapter 5, we address the wall of entitlement. As
Christians saved by grace (not by our merit), we are a blessed
people and thus there is no room for entitlement in the work
life of a Christian. But entitlement is insidious and can creep
in without our knowing it—so we need to grab hold of any
remaining entitlement and kill it. We are owed nothing and
given everything in Jesus. Entitlement cannot coexist with
grace which is, by nature, unmerited favor.

In Chapter 6, we dig into the wall of an increasingly secular
culture. The world is changing, and unless you're an ostrich,
you have noticed. In this chapter we look in depth at the trend
of the decline of Christianity and what that means for your 9
to 5. As the tide of culture moves away from the default mode
of a Judeo-Christian worldview, Christians will look more and
more like aliens. Our views and motives will be questioned,
and we need to know what we will do when we must choose
between our faith and cultural pressure.

In Chapter 7, we destroy the wall of perfectionism.
Perfectionism is darker than you think, though it cloaks itself
in hard work. At its root, perfectionism is a lack of trust in God
and perfectionists do not work faithfully—they work scared.
We need to let the grace of Christ wash over our perfectionism
and move on to work hard and get over ourselves.

In Chapter 8, we turn away from the walls and start to get
practical. What does it look like to lead faithfully? If we have
knocked down the walls between work and faith and have
become integrated people, how then do we lead others? That's
easy—we lead by serving. Jesus said the first shall be last, and

He washed the filth off of his friends' feet to show that leaders don't stand on their white horse and bark commands—they get on the ground and work alongside their team. Second, we show compassion to those we lead. We behave more like a parent than a boss, caring deeply not just for the work of our team but for their well-being. Finally, a Christ-like leader is curious and humble, always learning and always remembering his finite knowledge. Serve, lead, and learn.

In Chapter 9, we address the concept of tent-making. For those of us not involved in vocational ministry, does our work matter? How does work outside the church connect with serving God in ministry? First, our work can produce abundance, which allows us to tithe and empower the church through tithing. Second, our work affects our community, and we can bless our city and seek its welfare through our jobs. We must change our thinking from *having* to work to *getting* to work if we are going to work for the glory of God.

In Chapter 10, we wrap up by taking a look at the concept of time. We are given an eternity, and today is a part of that, but our lives on earth are finite. Each tick of the clock brings us closer to death, so we better make good use of our time. In this chapter we explore how to be effective with our time. We live in a unique time historically, with technology moving faster than we can comprehend. Those glowing pixelated boxes (phones, computers, TVs) can rob our time and thus keep us from doing great work if we aren't careful. Each day is a blessed opportunity to stand in joyful awe of our Creator.

At the end of each chapter, you will find a brief section of application. You see, ideas are great and all, but if they don't inspire action, they're not useful. So we'll start with new thinking and then turn that into new living. I encourage you to grab a journal or a piece of paper to write down your steps of application as you read the book. At the end of the book, I strongly encourage you to look back through your application exercises to pray through and think through the next steps for you to integrate your faith in Christ into your work. We must be doers, not just thinkers.

This book means the world to me, and I am grateful it has found its way into your hands. I pray that God would illuminate the words on the following pages in a way that only He can and that the upshot would be that your work and your faith would become one as we knock down walls together. As you integrate your work and faith, your joy will increase—trust me—and God will get truckloads of glory as He revolutionizes your relationship with your work life.

Chapter 1

GOD'S DESIGN FOR WORK

And God blessed them. And God said to them, "Be fruitful and multiply and fill the earth and subdue it, and have dominion over the fish of the sea and over the birds of the heavens and over every living thing that moves on the earth."

—Genesis 1:28

Let's start at the beginning. What does God say about this thing called "work?" If we establish a foundation of truth, we can then build upon it to help reshape our understanding of work.

How do you picture heaven? Are you playing a harp on a cloud or fishing for bass with your grandpa? Maybe you imagine (and hope for) roads made of bacon. We all have our mental pictures of heaven, each conforming to our desires. You see, our hopes form our expectation of what heaven will be like. We project our longings into our idea of heaven hoping they will be fulfilled. Isn't that what heaven should be—our longings satisfied? So let me ask you something—and let's be real here—is Jesus in your heaven? Picture a heaven without Him. Your family and friends are there and everything is paradise, except Jesus isn't there. Heaven minus Jesus.

Would you still want to go?

This question shocked me when I first heard it during a sermon by John Piper. It made me uneasy. I knew the answer I was supposed to give but honestly the question caught me flat-footed. The truth is that heaven without Jesus is hell. If we want heaven but not Jesus, we desire hell, as hell is by nature the separation of man from God. All of our longings ache empty without Jesus.

So what about our work? If our work has nothing to do with our faith in Christ—if it's just our "day job"—we are missing a giant chunk of our mission in life. We must bring our faith in Christ into our daily grind if we want to find meaning and joy in our work.

The presence of Jesus Himself (not just His stuff) must be our aim if we want to be happy. We can't run after the blessings of association with God; we must seek *Him*.

A recent Gallup poll found that nearly 70 percent of Americans are disengaged in their work.[1] That 70 percent equates to the population of Texas and California combined. The estimated economic cost of worker disengagement is in the hundreds of billions. Disengaged workers do not create beautiful work. They walk the line of minimum contribution and trying not to get fired. Statistically, there are lots of these folks in America, like 70 million of them. But why are these disengaged people so checked out? Do they have horrible bosses? Maybe. Are their companies a toxic environment? Perhaps. But it's deeper than that.

They lack a sense of *purpose.*

Say I hand Johnny a 50-pound bag of trash and ask him to carry it 25 miles. I don't tell him why—I just tell him I'll see him at the finish line. Unless Johnny thinks I've got something incredible for him when he finishes, he'll quit. Maybe he makes it to mile 5, but definitely not mile 10. Now what if I handed Johnny his injured daughter (who weighs 50 pounds) and said that the nearest hospital was 25 miles away? Only death could stop him. He'd have a *purpose* for his effort.

In Greek mythology, there's a guy named Sisyphus. He does something to make the gods mad. So the gods doom him to roll a rock to the top of a hill—and just as he reaches the top, it rolls back down. Up. Down. Up. Down. Forever. Meaningless. I think many of us Americans—well, statistically, 70 percent of us—feel like Sisyphus at work. Our lack of purpose drives a lack of engagement—which sucks the joy and fruitfulness out of our work.

The purpose is the lynchpin. As a Christian, I know that purpose had better come from God Himself, or I'm off course.

God rules every aspect of our lives. If you are a Christian, there is no part of your life where Jesus is not king. And He is a *good* king. Because we all want our work to mean something, we grow despondent when our work feels meaningless. Here's the thing—if we want our work to mean something, we need to put our work under the headship of Jesus. The Bible tells us quite a bit about work, and because Scripture reveals the ultimate truth, we should probably pay attention.

Work Is Good

After God created the earth, He created Adam and Eve. After He created Adam and Eve, He hired them. Genesis 1:28 contains the first blessing to Adam and Eve: welcome to the world, now *get to work*.

Remember, in Genesis 1 we are still in the Garden of Eden—the perfect place without sin or brokenness. Everything is just as God had made it, which is to say the whole world is perfect, like heaven. Since God commands (blesses) Adam and Eve to work even in this perfect world, God is making a huge statement here. This means that work is part of God's perfect plan for us. Work is a gift.

At this point in history, God calls everything on earth "good." Now God's definition of good is different than ours, or maybe the translators couldn't find the perfect word in English. We eat a good BLT on wheat; God creates good mountain peaks. When God calls something good, think awesome, amazing, incredible, mind-blowing. Be sure to elevate "good" when you see it written in Scripture.

Work is *good.*

Hold on just a minute. Am I saying that a miserable job is good? That depends on what you mean by "good." Your job may be downright awful, so how could it be that God designs work as good? This might seem inconsistent. Stay with me—we'll get there.

God works. He creates, sustains, and loves. He takes black nothing and makes it into bright something. He is forever on the move. As His children, we bear His image—thus, we have His work ethic in our DNA. In Genesis 2:5 we see that "there was no man to work the ground." This implies that God uses man to work the ground and this man was needed. Our work is part of His design, and when our hands are moving, we are fulfilling our first command from God. The absence of the working man (and woman) is a void which God sees fit to fill. We are His instruments to get stuff done.

Work was God's idea from the beginning. God made us to work.

Be Fruitful and Multiply

I don't know if you have kids, but I do. Two of them, a boy named Liam and a girl named Lila. And I love them so much my heart explodes. One time I asked Liam how much he loved me (you know that game: "How much do you love me?"), and he said, "I love you more than I can even tell you." I know what he means, because I can't properly express the love in my heart for my kids.

Strong love motivates action. We have to act upon love or else it isn't love, it's *like*. As Liam and Lila's parents, my wife and I don't merely feel warm affection—we pour out our lives for them. Our love causes us to act. God knew this dynamic (after all, He created it) when he told Adam and Eve to get out there and have kids. He knew that He was granting them an opportunity for deep love . . . and lots of work. This whole "be fruitful and multiply" business is no walk in the park. It's a call to hard work.

In case you don't know, raising kids is tiring. It starts with pregnancy, a nauseous hormone roller coaster. It's not comfortable to have another life growing inside you (so I hear). Then, childbirth. *Whoa, childbirth.* I was there for the birth of our two kids, and let's just say it was no cakewalk for Lindsay—and she's tough as nails. After the child is born, the real work begins. Parents spend all their time, energy, money, and sleep keeping their wriggling progeny alive. This is why new parents stagger around like they just went a few rounds with a silverback gorilla. Then the baby becomes a toddler, and life becomes controlled chaos. It's like combat with a bunch of plastic things that are made in China. The little humans can now move and break things, like themselves. It was no different in Adam and Eve's days; there were just different corners to babyproof. Just as work is a gift and kids are a gift (Psalm 127:3), raising kids is a gift. And it's hard.

Hard work and blessing are intertwined.

Taking Care of God's Stuff

After God gives the command to be fruitful and multiply, He tells Adam and Eve to take care of the earth. He tells them to have dominion over the plants and streams and . . . *everything.* Imagine the look on Adam's face when God told him to take care of the earth. Standing atop a mountain God points His finger and slowly turns in a circle.

"What do you see, Adam?"

"Uh. Is this a trick question, God? I see your world. Your kingdom."

"Indeed." (I think God says stuff like "indeed.") "Take care of it for me."

"Wait . . . me . . . how . . . um . . . okay?"

Now Adam and Eve couldn't buy a shovel with one click. The tractor wasn't invented. They wore plants for underwear, for crying out loud. Adam and Eve were in for some serious hard work stewarding God's creation. Yet the Bible says that God *blessed* them.

It's not that God couldn't take care of the earth. He spoke it into being. He sustains it all. No, what we have here is some divine delegation. God loves us enough to let us work and to care for His beautiful world. There's blessing in the work and there's work in the blessing. And He plays alongside us, bringing rain and progress.

Work is important to God. That's why it was His first blessing.

Something is Wrong Here

Why then do we have this strained relationship with work? We know we must do something on a daily basis that we call work, but it can be a real drag. Our disdain of work inspires movies like *Office Space*. In *Office Space*, Peter, the main character, hates his job. His useless TPS reports and his coffee-slurping boss drive him nuts. Peter decides to do something about it—he checks out. He still goes to work, but he is mentally disengaged (like 70 percent of Americans, apparently). The audience cheers Peter on as he moves deeper into brazen laziness. The movie is hilarious, and it resonates with us because we've all felt the monotony of a bad job.

What is up here? If God designed work as good and God doesn't fail, why do so many people loathe their jobs? We don't loathe the other things that God created as good, like sex and sunsets. When God designs something He doesn't create rat traps of disappointment.

To get an answer, we must move forward to Genesis 3. Genesis 1 to 2 contains a perfect world, absent of stain or sin or pain. God and man are physically together. Again, it's like heaven. But things take a turn for the terrible in Genesis 3 as sin enters perfection and fractures everything. Adam and Eve choose to turn their backs on God.

God tells Adam and Eve to run and play and enjoy The Garden. Then He warns them not to eat of a certain tree because it would kill them. Pretty easy to understand, right? But Satan tells Adam and Eve that God is holding out on them. He tells Adam and Eve that they won't die if they eat of the tree, and even better, they will be like God if they do—and they believe him. So they eat of the tree, turning their backs on God and embracing the fundamental lie of sin. Adam and Eve did this on purpose, using the freedom God granted them to turn away from Him. This wasn't just dipping into the cookie jar when God told them not to; it was cosmic treason. *No, I'll go my own way, thank you very much.*

This is called The Fall of Man. From this point forward, everything in the world changed for the worse, smeared black by sin. And hey, let's not get it twisted—we would have done the same thing Adam and Eve did. It's not that we inherit sin into our otherwise blameless lives because of our moron ancestors. We can't sit around and cuss our family tree, because we eat that stupid fruit every single day, choosing our way over God's way. Culpability for sin is as old as mankind. We all sin.

After The Fall, God cursed Adam and Eve and He cursed the earth. As a just and righteous God, He had to. Sin tipped the scales of justice and God had to right them. And herein lies the source of our problems with work: God cursed it. No longer would working in the (lowercase *g*) garden be working in The Garden.

God tells Adam,

> *Because you have listened to the voice of your wife and have eaten of the tree of which I commanded you, "You shall not eat of it," cursed is the ground because of you; in pain you shall eat of it all the days of your life; thorns and thistles it shall bring forth for you; and you shall eat the plants of the field. By the sweat of your face you shall eat bread, till you return to the ground.*
> —Genesis 3:17-19

Translation: *work is going to be hard.*

In Adam and Eve's time, the earth was new to them. Standing in The Garden, all was perfect, beautiful, and harmonious. You could literally bump into God on a walk. But in Genesis 3 the skies darken and things go down some kind of awful. Work was no longer like singing a song—now it was more like skateboarding over gravel. You know how it is—work is great for a season; you're sailing along going downhill, and then you hit one little pebble (your boss reprimands you unfairly, you turn something in late, or maybe you hear whispers of downsizing) and you find yourself banged up on the ground with skinned hands and knees. We work in a dichotomy: work is good but work is cursed.

Work is hard, whether you file TPS reports or dig ditches. Under the curse, we work "by the sweat of our face." It's not that hard work is bad or that work shouldn't be tiring. I am sure that before the curse Adam and Eve tuckered out after a long day in The Garden. But now we experience an exhaustion beyond putting in an honest day's work. Our energy reserves are short, which reduces our capacity and makes work frustrating. That's part of the curse.

Further, our work does not always produce the results we

hope for. That's the "thorns and thistles" curse at play. We work cursed ground.

Picture Adam and Eve. They find some seeds and plant them in the moist earth with their hands. Staring at the ground, they wait. "What will become of this little seed thing?" they wonder. Days later, a little sproutling pops up. Score! Adam runs to the little sproutling and gets down close to it. He pulls at it, hoping for a carrot, but instead grabs a handful of thorns. When the bills pile up while your bank account dwindles, that's thorns and thistles. When you leave the house one morning and end up standing on the porch at noon with a pink slip and a box full of your stuff from the office, that's thorns and thistles. You have been there, right? We have all felt the thorns and thistles of work.

It's tough out there. My buddy Kris says, "That's why they call it *work*." But this isn't the end of the story. We don't live in a Genesis 3 world—thank God. Let's keep moving.

The Turning Point

In case you didn't know, the Bible points to Jesus from cover to cover. As we move on from Genesis 3, there are plagues and wars and a bunch of people who can't keep God's commandments (we should relate well to these people). Try as they might, they cannot—we cannot—keep God's commands. And that's a real problem. When the Designer of the world tells us His world operates a certain way, and we do it our own way, it doesn't go well.

There is a trail of wreckage behind us.

But God . . .

At the right time, Jesus dove into the dark waters of this world to rescue us. He bore the weight of our sin on His shoulders so we could feel the warmth of His love on our life. Salvation has come—and salvation is a Person with nail-pierced hands. He saved us from ourselves, which is the gravest danger we face.

So what about our work? Did Jesus save us from that too?

Not exactly, but I have great news. For those of us who follow Jesus, we become more like Him every day. The Bible calls this process "sanctification." Tomorrow, you will be more like Jesus than you were today. But sanctification is not a fixed linear progression (picture a straight line on a graph). We can do something about the speed at which we become like Christ (picture an upward sloping line on a graph). That's why you can meet a Christ-like 25 year old and a spiritually childish 70 year old. The 25 year old has probably spent more time seeking Jesus and thus has changed rapidly while maybe the 70 year old has just drifted through life like a leaf in a curbside trickle.

I used to be able to do a back roll on a wakeboard behind a boat. If I tried today I might be a life insurance claim, but I could do it back in the day. Anyway, if you want to do a back roll, you need to use your eyes. As you cut into the boat's wake and become airborne, you look up and behind you—and your body follows. Your body follows your eyes. So too our soul follows our gaze—we become what we behold. So if we behold the subpar (money, fame, popularity), we'll become a jacked-up semblance of our idol. Likewise, if we behold Jesus we will experience progressive sanctification at a good clip. And our work will follow this pattern of redemption.

We are the agents of work, meaning our hands are the ones doing the work, and thus the person behind the work is the pivot point. An oversimplified formula is this: bad person = bad work; good person = good work. Because of the work of Jesus in our sinful hearts, as sanctified workers growing in grace our work is on the path to redemption.

I have a hypothesis: I think we will work in heaven. The new heaven and new earth combined will look a lot like The Garden (except we know from Scripture that it'll be a city). Purity, beauty, harmony, and *work*. You see, God is meticulous. The first blessing to Adam and Eve means something. So I reckon we'd better get used to the idea of work and get our minds right, because we'll never retire. Isaiah 65:22-23 offers a peek behind the curtain of redeemed work:

> *They shall not build and another inhabit; they shall not plant and another eat; for like the days of a tree shall the days of my people be, and my chosen shall long enjoy the work of their hands. They shall not labor in vain or bear children for calamity, for they shall be the offspring of the blessed of the LORD, and their descendants with them.*

So yeah, we'll work in heaven. And it will be fruitful, productive, and joyful. We are already on this road, even though we have a long way to go. Look ahead and let this promise motivate your work. Who knows what cool stuff we'll create and build in heaven?

Let's start down that joyful path today.

We must be careful, though. If we pursue a relationship with Jesus merely because of His power and not because we love Him, we are playing games with God and trying to cheat the system. And God doesn't play games. The aim is the person of Christ. Otherwise we're barking up the wrong tree. (For a great example of this going some kind of awful, see how this goes for the Jewish exorcists in Acts 19:11-17.)

Economists have a term called positive externality. A positive externality is a benefit extending beyond the micro level of a decision. The benefit is not the primary reason for the decision—it's a bonus. For example, if we work hard we will be more successful, and this benefits us. Our benefit is what we are working for. But a positive externality of hard work is that society benefits as well. If we have enough money for healthcare, we are less likely to carry illness to other people and to depend upon others for help. If our business grows, we can hire more people. The tide of human flourishing rises, and less people live in poverty as a positive externality of hard work.

A positive externality of following Jesus is that all areas of our life follow Him and are influenced by His grace and power, including our work. There is no sacred/secular divide. Let me say that again: there is no sacred/secular divide. There is no secular work—just work. There is no secular music—just music. God will have His glory in all things, not just what we deem sacred. That is what drove me crazy during my early career—the accepted assumption that faith and work are in different worlds. There is just one world and one God and thus, like everything else, work is under God's headship.

As you follow Jesus and begin to mold to Him, your work follows.

Walking Through Walls

When I was a boy, we lived in the country for a while. We had a barn and horses and a red Massey Ferguson tractor. I would take my pellet gun, head to the creek behind our house, and explore and shoot things for hours. The creek was copper from the clay bottom, and the humidity glued your shirt to your skin. The trees were thick and so were the bugs and snakes. It was a boy's paradise.

This one day I went exploring with a friend. We ventured far down the creek and followed some offshoot tributaries. We scrambled along crumbly ledges lining the creek, trying not to fall in. (We failed on purpose.) Hours passed. It was hot and we grew tired and we were far away from home—at least in kid distance. We looked up and couldn't figure out which forks to take to get back. We were lost. I remember the feeling of dread that came over me in that moment. We had no food, no water, and no plan to get home. This all sounds dramatic now—you could have hit a golf ball from our pasture to where I was—but I didn't know that at the time. So there I was, feeling lost and scared.

I don't know about you, but I sometimes still feel lost in

the world, far away from home. I confess that in my work I sometimes feel like that lost little boy again, wondering how it will all pan out. *Which way is home?*

God is so gracious to give us Scripture to explain what we need to know and to lead us home to Him. He does not tell us everything, just what He wants us to know. Apparently, He wants us to know that work is hard, but it is on the path to redemption, which is the path to Himself. We know which road to take to get home if we walk behind Jesus and seek after Him. God offers hope in this good news.

TAKE ACTION

Reflection: What old views about work do you need to let go? What new understandings do you need to grab hold of? Write these down.

Prayer: We need God's help here. If we are going to reorient our hearts as we work, we need the Spirit to draw near and shape our thinking and affections. Pray to God and ask Him for help to integrate your faith into work. Ask Him to show you what He has for you in work. (Write this down and keep it available. Remember, we'll go over your application at the end of the book.)

Action: New understanding should create new living. The next time you are about to go to work—whatever that means for you—stop. Don't rush into the day and start answering emails and running like a mad person. Take a second to stop, close your eyes, and thank God for the gift of work. Ask Him for His help and guidance.

Chapter 2

FAITH INTO WORK

My soul magnifies the Lord.
—Luke 1:46

Now that we understand God's design for work, sin's impact on work, and the positive trajectory of work (because of sanctification in Christ), let's take a closer look at what integrated faith and work looks like. It is crucial to visualize the desired outcome with any endeavor, so let's do that here with our work.

Jesus reigns over all of life, not just our time in the pews on Sunday. His territory is endless. This means we don't have a work life and a spiritual life—we just have a life.

For whatever reason—probably because of The Fall—our default mode is to segment our lives into categories. While having a beer with our buddies, we are vulgar and tough, but before the communion altar we are misty-eyed reverent. And part of this is understandable, because certain contexts call for different parts of our personality. But what is important here is not that we use the same default behavior at all times, but rather that our every breath is authentically in sync with what we deem to be most important. This is the true measure of authenticity or "being true to yourself," as they say. Moods and behaviors vary based upon the situation at the time, but we must proceed from the bedrock of transcendent truth. We may change, but the truth does not. And we must do our best to anchor our hearts upon God's truth.

Work is important, as we established in the preceding chapter, but work is not the pinnacle of life. We must integrate our faith in Christ into our jobs, not because our jobs are of supreme importance, but because Jesus is—and our career is another way to experience Him.

Here's a gut check. If I were to film your day, what would the video show about your priorities? What would the viewer say you deem most important? Money? Stuff? Vacations? Leisure? Three fingers of single malt? Where does your mind drift during idle times? What do your social media feeds, credit card bills, and friends say you value the most?

The condition of the heart is what matters. In case that sounds a little vague or hard to pin down, let me say that the *affections* of your heart matter. Your desires, wants, and hungers all point to the condition of your heart. Though Christians are a living dichotomy of sin and righteousness, a heart redeemed in Christ will, by the power of the Spirit, drive the affections toward Him. If your heart holds no affections for Jesus, it won't do you much good to integrate Him into your job. You don't need to graduate to some higher echelon of Christianity (those don't exist)—you just need to make sure you are a Christian to begin with. That's step one. (If this subject makes you uneasy, remember that per 1 Timothy 2:4 God desires that all be saved. You are not chasing a unicorn. If you desire salvation you are feeling the effectual call of the Holy Spirit. Repent of your sin and believe.)

Let's be real—we all sell out on a daily basis. We choose creation over the Creator and eat from the tree of our own way, which is the essence of sin. I know that way too often I get off course and have to reorient myself toward Jesus. He saves me from myself. Just remember as you go on this journey of faithful work that true north is Jesus—any other path falls short. And you will have to reorient yourself at times because you're a normal, sinful human.

Okay, let's move forward. So what does it look like to integrate faith in Jesus into our work?

Working Faithfully

Colossians 3:23 reminds us that whatever we do, we should do so as if we are working for God. That means if you shovel manure, you had best be the best manure scooper the world has ever seen—or at least you should try.

In a 1981 sermon, John Piper said, "God is very much more concerned with the way you do the job that you now have than he is with whether you get a new job."[2] Amen. Too many of us think *if only* when God just calls us to be fruitful today. 1 Corinthians 7:17 says that God assigns us a life, and our occupation certainly falls within that category. So our jobs are an assignment from God. Now they aren't a permanent assignment (we aren't given a life sentence to our job), but if we marry 1 Corinthians 7:17 with Matthew 6:34 (paraphrase: don't be anxious about tomorrow—worry about today), we have a clear command to make the best of our current gig, no matter what we think of it. Work hard and trust that God placed you right where you are.

Too often we hear the mantra that we need to follow our passion. The problem is that our hearts are deceitful (Jeremiah 17:9) and make a poor compass, so our passions are just the outworking of a deceitful organ. Also, I have seen many folks follow their passion to their couch so they can talk about their great ideas and play video games. Meanwhile, everyone else is at work.

I do believe in following your passion and chasing your dreams, by the way. I think that's great. But this mindset can shoot the wheels off of our work lives if we aren't careful. If we forget that work itself is the gift (not just a means to an end), we'll miss the point of work. Dreams are flighty and passions change. We need something a little more stable to hold on to: a *mission*.

As Christians in the workplace, *our mission is to magnify the Lord and bring Him honor*. The work of our hands should testify to the greatness of God.

One important component of faithful, missional work is boldness. Our work—whatever it is—should stand out as bold and beautiful. You see, we have the Spirit of God living in us, so the work of our hands should reflect Him. Our work should be beautiful. Your work may seem mundane, though. Say you're an auto mechanic and all you see is grease and tools and cars. You can't see how your work could or should be beautiful. What does beautiful work look like under the hood of a Volvo? The beauty is in the execution of the work, and not always the end result of the work. Here is what I mean: if you, the mechanic, work with such skill and diligence that you repair your customer's vehicle quickly and for a decent price, you have performed your craft beautifully. The customer probably cannot see their repaired transmission, but they can see you—and a skilled mechanic taking a broken vehicle and putting it back on the road is a beautiful thing. You are repairing a broken part of someone's life.

Looking again to 1 Corinthians 7:17, we see that God assigns us a life, meaning God put us in our today. He does not wonder how on earth we got to an insurance agency in Liberal, Kansas. Do you want to know how you're living the life God has planned for you? You're living. He is sovereign, and if He wanted you somewhere else, He would put you somewhere else.

Do your job. And do it to the best of your ability. You may not have your job forever, but it's the one you have today.

Nothing to Lose

God knows the number of hairs on our heads. His eternal arms hold our momentary lives. He knows our fears and our worries, our tears and our apprehensions. He is *involved*. Your life isn't foreign to Him—He made it, and He's shaping it.

God's involvement in our life means we can take bold risks in our careers. If God is for us, who can be against us? Well, actually a lot of people can and will be against us. But they cannot thwart what God is doing nor can anything (or anyone) separate us from the love of Christ (Romans 8:38-39). We are spiritually secure. Fear will still nip at our heels and breathe its breath on our necks telling us to shut up, they're all going to laugh, but faithfulness means pushing on anyway, knowing that God is in control and He cares for us.

Don't overthink things—just go.

Because of our spiritual security in Jesus, Christians should be the biggest risk takers at work. If we truly believe what we say we believe—that Jesus is our Savior and that He is our everything—we should be free to risk big because we already have our everything. The most beautiful art is produced by risk. Launching a new business carries risk. And so on. All meaningful work is risky, even if it is just ordinary work performed extraordinarily. If you want to produce great work, you will need to dive into risk, look fear in the face, and square your shoulders. God will meet you there.

Recently I climbed a mountain with my dad. Two, actually. We climbed Guadalupe Peak, which is literally the top of Texas. I researched the climb to Guadalupe Peak and wasn't intimidated. The climb was rated strenuous but based on the reports from people who had made the summit it seemed more like a long hike than a challenging mountain climb. I saw pictures of AARP members snapping photos on the peak, so it didn't appear to be much of a challenge. All this swagger from a dude who had never climbed a mountain.

Our friend Deryl told us you could turn the ascent to Guadalupe Peak into another climb to a different peak called El Capitan. That makes for two peaks in one day. El Capitan is attached to Guadalupe Peak by a steep saddle, and you can bushwhack your way from Guadalupe to El Capitan, so we were told. We would soon learn what "bushwhack" entails. Deryl said that we would have to climb El Capitan and that this bonus climb would make it all worth it. He said that everything in us would make us want to turn back, but we should keep going no matter what. Dad and I are down for a challenge—especially together—so we were all in.

We made it to the top of Texas. Sitting on top of Guadalupe Peak, we felt good. We scarfed down some peanut butter and honey sandwiches and chugged water. We took pictures and sat down for a moment after the three-hour summit to our first peak. After we had rested for about 10 minutes, we got up, packed our gear, pulled out our climbing poles, and put on gloves (the gloves made us look more legitimate if nothing else). We walked back down the trail as if to descend Guadalupe, except we made a hard right and started going down the face of Guadalupe toward El Capitan. It was steep, loose, and unstable. I am sure that anyone who saw us do this thought we were either experienced climbers (false) or idiots (true).

As we descended we checked on each other, and we both said we were fine. Onward. Finally, we picked our way through a steep rocky swale to the bottom of the saddle and looked up at several peaks, not knowing which was *the* peak. *Uh, that one.* We started to climb, one leg at a time. Plant leg, plant climbing pole, push climbing pole into the ground, and step up. Repeat.

We climbed in a diagonal pattern, creating what climbers call switchbacks (basically a zig-zag trail). Suddenly, Dad blurted a cornucopia of profanity and leaped like a ballerina. I don't remember what he said, but the end of his outburst was "SNAKE!"

He pointed down at where his feet were just seconds before his leap. A four-foot rattlesnake lay outstretched on the ground, its tongue licking the air nonchalantly. His boot had touched the side of the snake as he planted his foot. Thankfully, this was a pretty chill snake.

We took some pictures of our new friend, our hearts in our throats, then moved on. If dad had been bitten, he would be dead. We had no cell service, I had no way to get help, and that old cowboy crap of lancing the snakebite and sucking out venom would probably not have ended well. (Don't do that, by the way.) By God's grace we continued toward the top of El Capitan, scared to death. Every square inch of the mountain looked like a snake. It made for slow going.

But we had to keep going.

We somehow made it to the peak, and Dad lay down to kiss the summit register box. The wind whipped at our shirts, and we sat feet from death because that's where you sit on top of a mountain. Dad had just slid past death with the snake encounter on the trail, and now we sat feet from death. We clung to the ground tightly.

We made it down the mountain eventually, tired yet wired. And it was worth the risk and the sweat.

In our careers, we should look for El Capitan moments. Moments where you're in new territory, rife with risk. Moments where fear is bigger than motivation. If you are mission-driven instead of emotion-driven, you'll remember that your job is bigger than you. You'll remember that, as George Patton once said, "A good plan, violently executed now, is better than a perfect plan next week."[3] So execute violently right now, even if you're scared. Don't give into a spirit of fear (Romans 8:15).

Working faithfully means putting one foot in front of the other with bold trust in God—especially when the path is unsure and littered with rattlesnakes. God's arm is not too short to save you. Fear is inevitable, but faith shoves fear off the trail so you can keep moving. We have to move through fear, not around it.

Working faithfully requires . . . *faith*. Faith in the things we hope for and the belief that hope is there even when we can't see it. But most importantly, our faith is rooted in the hope of what Jesus has already done for sinners like us. The promises of Christ were fulfilled when Jesus walked out of the grave. In Christ we have assurance of everything we hope for, and this should give us conviction for our mission of work. It should keep us going.

God does not have you somewhere else. He has you right where you are this very moment, reading this book. And He means for you to do something with this moment. Work faithfully.

Sharing Your Faith

Our lives must be the greatest testament to the truth and beauty of Christ. Actions do indeed speak louder than words. But if we want to share the truth of the Gospel with other people at work, we will need to capitalize on the opportunity to use words.

Paul explains in Hebrews,

> *How then will they call on him in whom they have not believed? And how are they to believe in him of whom they have never heard? And how are they to hear without someone preaching?*
>
> —*Romans 10:14*

Theodore Roosevelt once said, "People don't care how much you know until they know how much you care." That sounds like a nice saying to put on a coffee mug above the head of a cat sleeping on a pillow, but stay with me. If we authentically care about our colleagues and clients, love will set the stage for conversations of eternal significance. If we treat people like a means to an end, they will notice and recoil. People are smart like that and they can sense motive like a deer senses rain. We must focus on the *conversation* and let God worry about the *conversion*.

When I was in college, my buddies and I would play pick-up basketball games for hours. Well there was this guy. He always wore cut off t-shirts with Bible verses scrawled all over them in permanent marker. I don't know how many of those shirts he made but he had plenty. When he played in a game, he would get the ball and jack up three-pointers with maybe a 10-percent shooting percentage. I didn't want him on my team, nor did anyone else. After games, he would walk around to people with an evangelistic script akin to a sales script for selling kitchen knives. People would scatter like cockroaches.

One time he cornered me as I was leaving the Rec Center. I was sweaty and exhausted and about to get some water from the water fountain. As he walked up, I knew what was about to go down. So I tried to head him off. As he began his spiel, I nodded in agreement and said something like, "Yeah man, I feel you. I know Jesus too." Thankfully this was enough, and he went on to other people.

My point is not to make fun of this guy. Not at all. For a young man in college, he was surprisingly zealous and bold, and I appreciate the child-like nature of his evangelism. He believed in Jesus and wanted other people to know Him too—so he just got after it. But I believe his approach could have been much more effective if he had worked to build a relationship or maybe just a level of mutual respect. (And, bro, if you are reading this, please pass the ball.)

Years ago I would sprinkle God into conversations at the office as if He were a name to drop. "Yeah, isn't it great that we got that account? *God is good*." You know, trite interjections. It was as if saying God's name was a gospel presentation, except I knew it wasn't because every time I tried this tactic it felt contrived and a little stupid. I just didn't know what else to say.

It's awkward to share your faith at work. It's uncouth. But it need not be forced and weird. The simple solution is to tell our story and to learn about the stories of others. What has Jesus done in your life? What did He rescue you from? What does your faith mean to you? You see, we aren't debating here. The goal isn't to argue your coworker to faith (that's impossible); it's to invite them into a life of meaning—to lead them to the fountainhead of eternal life.

Words about Jesus have no texture or meaning if our lives do not reinforce the ideas which we espouse. For example, if we preach humility yet are ego mongers, we betray our words. Character and a faithful life must undergird our faith at work.

A while back I sat down with my friend Kris over a cigar. As we sat and smoked on his porch, we talked about how challenging it is to break down the wall between work and faith. Kris explained that one of the higher-ups at his company did something practical and powerful: he invited people to a Bible study. I know this may seem obvious, but sometimes the wise things in life are smack-you-in-the-face simple.

I gave this a shot shortly after we had this conversation. I invited my team of three (myself included, I said yes) to sit down over lunch and study Ephesians. One guy said yes and the other said no thanks. The Bible study was not a roaring success; it was spotty and sporadic. But you know what, this simple invitation helped bridge the gap between daily work and my relationship with Jesus. It brought me and the guy who said yes closer as well. It was a step forward.

We aren't paid to evangelize our coworkers, though. We are paid to work. We have a job to do. If sharing your faith is inappropriate and keeps you from doing the work you were hired for, get back to work. Opportunities will come as God sees fit.

If we aim to connect our faith and work, we'll need to share our faith and to come out of the closet as a Christian. Preach the gospel always, and it's necessary to use words.

It's about What Jesus Has Done

Working faithfully is less about what you can do and more about what Jesus has done. His faithful execution of His work empowers and inspires our faithful execution of ours. When we look upon the cross of Christ and taste His redemption, we will be filled to the brim with hope. And this hope should compel us to work with faith and trust. Furthermore, if we carry the treasure of the Gospel with us, we will be unable to remain quiet. By God's grace, our life will be a testament to the One who saved us and raised us from death in sin.

When you trust Jesus, you can work without fear. You can also carry out your tasks with the assurance that you are forgiven, saved, and redeemed. This assurance breeds great execution, which breeds great work. And again, when your heart is bursting with hope, you'll share that hope with those around you.

But we still have walls that get in the way. We have insecurities and external factors that make integrated work difficult. These walls are a real problem, but the great news is that when we pour the truth of God over them, they cannot contain us.

Let's get to work on those walls.

TAKE ACTION

Reflection: In Christ we have everything we need. Do you believe that? What would a deeper satisfaction in Jesus mean for your work life? Would this change the way you see risk or how you face fear in your vocation? Write down your answers.

<u>Prayer</u>: What you call work is unique to you. You have different tasks, experiences, and people than even your coworkers. So there is no uniform strategy to integrate God into the work of your hands. Ask the Lord to show you what He has for you in your work. Write down your prayer.

<u>Action</u>: In Chapter 1 we started with thankfulness. Let's build upon that thankfulness. Today as you consider your work, when moments of trial, discomfort, and difficulty arise—no matter how small—pour the promises of Jesus over them. Preach the Gospel to yourself, remembering that Jesus has saved you from your sins, He loves you, and all things work together for good for those who love God (Romans 8:28). Trust this promise.

Chapter 3

WALL 1:
GET YOUR MIND RIGHT
ABOUT MONEY

*No one can serve two masters, for either he will hate the
one and love the other, or he will be devoted to the one and
despise the other. You cannot serve God and money.*
—Matthew 6:24

The first wall we must get through is a misunderstanding
of money. Most of us have some reorienting to do in
regards to a biblical understanding of money. And
reorient we must, as wrong thinking leads to wrong acting,
because what we believe guides our lives. This is why theology
is so important; we must hold the right truths in our heart.

Before we can move on, we need to start with a basic theology
of money. I will not go in depth like a seminary class because
I didn't go to seminary. As a regular working guy, I hope to
present the theology of money in a simple and clear manner.

Many of us hold tightly to worldly promises that are not

grounded in biblical truth. Maybe that's why our hearts keep getting broken. God seems to ignore these promises—because He never made them. We are playing the game of life and work by a different set of rules than God intended. Money is no exception.

The end result of our work is usually money. We work to get a paycheck. Now, hopefully our motivation goes deeper than that (and I hope to convince you of deeper motivation of work), but we need to take a look at the carrot we chase with our daily work. If we don't understand money, our work will suffer. We have got to address this wall of misunderstanding money so we can walk through it.

The point of this chapter is to warn you. Bad theology of money will not only keep you from connecting your faith and work, but it will also keep you from Jesus. He said so. This money stuff matters.

I want to talk about two poles on the spectrum of money theology that affect your work: the prosperity gospel and the poverty gospel.

The Prosperity Gospel

The prosperity gospel tricks its followers and leads them by the hand down a rose-covered path to a lie. The lie is that God's will for you is to be rich and live a perfect life—right now on earth. Just pray harder, tithe more; come on, pray harder!

Churches preaching the prosperity gospel thrive everywhere: poor, affluent, white, black. The message is a version of the same promise, and the promise is essentially heaven on earth right now. That's a pretty attractive message, isn't it? That whole dying to get to heaven thing sounds scary, but heaven right now sounds a little better. Plus, for some reason, the prosperity gospel pimps seem to drive really nice cars.

God does wish for us to prosper and to be happy. It is His plan for us (Jeremiah 29:11). But true flourishing is found in a relationship with God Himself, not just His blessings. He gives His blessings (like money) in different measures to different people, but for those of us that seek Him, He pours His love and presence like a waterfall. Prosperity is measured in your soul, not your bank account.

Furthermore, we aren't in heaven. Scripture is quite clear on that. You know how you know we aren't in heaven? Jesus isn't physically here hanging out with us. We aren't in our Father's house (John 14:2). Only a fool would mistake this world for the heaven promised in Scripture.

The prosperity gospel is not innocent foolishness—it is a deadly trick.

When you forego Jesus as your treasure, you put something else in His place. That's called idolatry. When you put money in His place (or happiness, or wellness, or whatever) you prop up a lie where an Eternal Savior should be. Your life guided by anything other than Jesus is a tragedy, but a life guided by money is a train wreck.

The prosperity gospel ignores a fundamental tenet of the Christian faith: suffering. The doctrine of suffering is central to the life of the Christian. We will endure suffering, persecution, and hardship. Paul explains in 1 Peter 4:12,

Beloved, do not be surprised at the fiery trial when it comes upon you to test you, as though something strange were happening to you.
                                                                —1 Peter 4:12

Suffering is not an anomaly—it is the norm. Prolonged prosperity and safety (as we currently have in the United States) is the exception to the rule. We live in a jacked-up and broken world, and at some point the brokenness will converge upon our lives. But the great news about trials is that God uses suffering like a paintbrush to display His great love and glory. He uses suffering to create hope and forge our character:

Not only that, but we rejoice in our sufferings, knowing that suffering produces endurance, and endurance produces character, and character produces hope, and hope does not put us to shame, because God's love has been poured into our hearts through the Holy Spirit who has been given to us.
—Romans 5:3-5

Sellers (and yes, they are selling something) of the prosperity gospel will either remain silent on suffering or will explain that suffering is an obstacle we just have to get around. The solution tends to be connected to you having more faith and giving to their ministry. But suffering is part of God's redemptive plan, and His plans will come to fruition. It did not go well for the apostles, many of whom were imprisoned and tortured to death for their faith in Jesus. John the Baptist was the greatest man in history, according to Jesus Himself—and John had his head chopped off. Paul wrote much of the New Testament, and much of our knowledge about God came through his pen—and Paul was beaten and imprisoned frequently. These mighty men of God did not find material prosperity in the world, but their hearts were overflowing with the joy of Christ.

The other day I watched a video compilation of prosperity gospel preachers from the 80s and 90s. I was enthralled and disgusted at the same time. The common thread with these guys (aside from big hair) is that all of them were desperate and mad. Their gaudy TV sets behind them, they railed on and on and shared "words from God"—and for some reason God spoke to them only when it resulted in their making more money. One guy promised money from God if you sent him money. He didn't feel the need to cloak his plan very well, I guess. These dudes are hucksters.

You have suffered. I know you have. I know that this broken world has closed in on you through the death of a loved one or through sickness. You've lost jobs, buried loved ones, and struggled. You have been rejected. Suffering spares no one.

As Christians we are blessed to suffer with purpose, with joy. We can even rejoice in our suffering, hard as it may be (Romans 5:3-5). It's coming, so we might as well figure out how to make the best of it. This isn't masochism or pessimism; it's just God's honest truth. And the fun part about all of this is that while suffering hurts, the gospel does sell an abundant life. This abundant life cannot be crushed by bankruptcy or even death. The abundance is in a deep, abiding, forever relationship with Jesus Christ Himself—and suffering makes your bond only stronger. This puts us in a *can't lose* situation. The treasure of a relationship with Jesus cannot be compared to trifles like money, power, fame, and other temporary things that promise joy.

A relationship with Jesus will lead you down thorny paths—but He will always be with you on that path.

The Washington Post called the prosperity gospel one of the worst ideas of the decade. I think it might be one of the worst ideas in human history. In an opinion column titled "The Worst Ideas of the Decade: The Prosperity Gospel," Cathleen Falsani writes,

> *Jesus was born poor, and he died poor. During his earthly tenure, he spoke time and again about the importance of spiritual wealth and health. When he talked about material wealth, it was usually part of a cautionary tale.*[4]

"Gospel" means good news. Because the prosperity gospel is a big fat lie, it is really no gospel at all. It certainly isn't good news. It is a great way to fill up a church and to sell books, but the preachers pile up promises into a house of cards that will collapse onto the congregation when the truth comes out in the circumstances of life.

Don't be left standing under this house of cards. Get some real promises.

If you go through your work life thinking your destiny is to be rich, you'll become a lover and chaser of money. An addict even. And your tolerance will increase, just like an addict. What used to satisfy you will become the minimum effective dose. The pursuit of money is an endless race with no winner and no finish line.

Jesus says you can't serve God and money. If you ignore this clear warning from the One who loves you most, you'll be saying, "Okay, Jesus, that's cool. I'll go with money." You will, in the spirit of pursuing "God's will for your life," chase money hard. You will work yourself to the bone because, in your seemingly innocent quest toward the will of God, you are just doing what you're supposed to. That's what your big-haired pastor said, right?

We will be sell outs—either to Jesus or to money. Our worship will clearly show our heart's highest value, and we all worship. It's just a matter of what or whom.

Hear the words of author David Foster Wallace on the object of our worship:

Because here's something else that's weird but true: in the day-to-day trenches of adult life, there is actually no such thing as atheism. There is no such thing as not worshipping. Everybody worships. The only choice we get is what to worship. And the compelling reason for maybe choosing some sort of god or spiritual-type thing to worship—be it JC or Allah, be it YHWH or the Wiccan Mother Goddess, or the Four Noble Truths, or some inviolable set of ethical principles—is that pretty much anything else you worship will eat you alive. If you worship money and things, if they are where you tap real meaning in life, then you will never have enough, never feel you have enough. It's the truth. Worship your body and beauty and sexual allure and you will always feel ugly. And when time and age start showing, you will die a million deaths before they finally grieve you. On one level, we all know this stuff already. It's been codified as myths, proverbs, clichés, epigrams, parables; the skeleton of every great story. The whole trick is keeping the truth up front in daily consciousness.[5]

Now, as far as I know, David Foster Wallace was not a Christian. He is not saying from a Christian perspective that we should worship Jesus because all other objects of worship "will eat you alive." Though he didn't cite the Bible as the source, Wallace is espousing a profound biblical truth that worshiping a non-spiritual thing is like drinking spiritual poison.

"We will die a million deaths . . ."

If you worship money, you will get neither God nor enough money. There is not enough money to fill the cavernous hole in our hearts that an eternally-loving God should fill. The richest people in the world are often on the same treadmill of anxiety as the rest of us—if not to a greater extent. They just cry in their helicopters while we cry in our well-worn Toyotas.

We know that in Genesis 3 God tells us that the ground is cursed. Thorns and thistles it shall bring forth. One consequence of the thorns and thistles curse is that money is hard to come by. And we know the gritty reality of life proves the thorns and thistles reality. Most of us have experienced a time when we're short on cash.

Now, it is quite possible to become wealthy if you work hard over a long period of time and save your money. Hustle is effective and thrift is wise. Proverbs has plenty to say about this topic. Making money—even truckloads of it—is not the problem.

The issue is the condition of our hearts, which is directly related to where we place our trust.

Jesus said it's easier for a camel to go through the eye of a needle than for a rich person to enter heaven. This is one of those brilliant word pictures Jesus uses. Can you imagine a camel going through the eye of a needle?

Maybe you're rich, with a huge portfolio of equities and investments and cash for a rainy day. It doesn't mean you're

going to hell. It doesn't mean Jesus doesn't love you and that
you have to figure out how to get a camel through the eye of a
needle just because you're well off. Jesus is warning us because
money is like a leech—you wade into the water to play and leave
the water with blood-suckers. The love of money gets all over
us. Our hearts love to idolize money and Jesus knew that, which
is why He tells us to be careful. Be careful that we value nothing
over Him.

Money draws out our heart's desires like an industrial strength
magnet. For example, if you really just want to be noticed, your
money will serve you in this endeavor by giving you the slickest
car, the coolest watch, the biggest house, and the most stylish
clothes. People will look at you and give you attention—mission
accomplished. Money will get you attention.

Or maybe your deepest desire is for intimacy. Maybe you
just want to be loved and appreciated and wanted. Your money
can buy you friends or hookers in that case, both just hanging
with you because of your money and both leaving when your
usefulness to them is done. In such a case there would be two
victims: you for using them and them for using you. It's a one-
for-one exchange of abuse. You'll know it and so will they, but
at least you're throwing water on top of your burning heart. Or
gasoline. (When we use other people we both end up used, but
when we serve other people we both end up served.)

You see, money can play a decent little god for a little while,
tickling our desires. But it never gets to the root of the desire.
Because we are eternal beings, our deepest desires are fixed
upon the transcendent, the eternal. Filling an eternal hunger
with temporary food is like slowly starving someone to death
by giving them one Skittle per day until they die.

Yes, money can prop us up for quite a while if we have a
bunch of it. It can keep us distracted and busy and amused. But
eventually we'll pay the piper when the money runs out or when
death knocks its bony hand on the door of our ostentatious
house. This game doesn't last.

If you put your faith in the prosperity gospel, you'll walk around like you're suffocating. You won't have the reward promised by the prosperity gospel, and you will think you are starving spiritually. And you will be, but not just because you don't have enough money.

If we treat money as simply a store of value, neither moral nor immoral, and just work hard and diligently, we may find that God will bless us with money. In fact, the odds are pretty good. And if we check our hearts and help ground ourselves in the truth that God wants us to be happy in Him—and not just in His stuff—when money does come we will find it to be a blessing.

Be vigilant when someone's interpretation of Scripture revolves around piling up money. True prosperity is found in the treasure of Jesus Christ.

The Poverty Gospel

Now let's talk about the opposite of the prosperity gospel, the poverty gospel. The message of the poverty gospel is subversive, and it's a little easier to think *hmmm, that makes sense*—so we need to be careful. The poverty gospel is quiet and stands there with its hands in its pockets telling you not to mind it. It's just poor little old me.

The poverty gospel says that God's will for you is to be poor and destitute, your wrinkled paper cup outstretched to passersby. The poverty gospel is justified in the minds of its adherents by the fact that Jesus Himself was poor and homeless for much of His life. With Jesus as our example, shouldn't we follow suit? Jesus being the God-man didn't exactly have to be poor.

No, He did not. Jesus was very intentional in His life and ministry. Jesus' being poor was certainly on purpose. But Jesus' lack of money is not a blanket commandment for all of us to be poor.

So why did Jesus choose to be poor?

1. <u>His poverty spoke to His humility</u>. Jesus was not a great-looking guy and He didn't have money. Consider the following verse in Isaiah:

> *For he grew up before him like a young plant,*
> *and like a root out of dry ground;*
> *he had no form or majesty that we should look at him,*
> *and no beauty that we should desire him.*
> —*Isaiah 53:2*

   Jesus could have come to earth in wild riches, making others desire Him for His money and His looks. Like too many paintings, Jesus could have had long, blond, flowing locks and Greek-statue arms. But He chose to be poor and plain-looking as an act of pure humility.

2. <u>A poor king is an oxymoron</u>. Jesus was countercultural. He liked blowing up stereotypes. The Pharisees hated Him for this. A homeless guy walking around saying He was the Son of God would have given people cause for doubt and unbelief—and that's just what happened. Jesus made a bold statement with his poverty.

3. <u>Jesus wanted to relate to us</u>. Most of us aren't millionaires. Jesus sat with lepers and ate dinner with "those people" (us) of society, and for Him to do so as a rich guy would have seemed patronizing. Jesus was a blue collar guy—someone you could sit down with over a cold beer.

4. <u>Jesus needed to say something about money</u>. Though He had a very rough life and a heinous death, Jesus went to the cross "for the joy set before Him." Jesus

had little money but He had joy in His relationship with His Father. (Now the Bible does refer to Him as a "man of sorrows," as He went through a tragically painful and difficult life—but joy is beyond circumstance when it's rooted in God.) Joy is rooted in hope, and Jesus knew the other end of His suffering was communion with the Father and the Holy Spirit. Jesus showed us that we can have joy without money, even in the midst of great suffering.

The poverty gospel almost fits with the life of Jesus, but not quite if you're paying attention. God doesn't call us to be rich, and He doesn't call us to be poor. He calls us to live the life He assigned to us (1 Cor. 7:17) and to get busy loving Him and other people.

If we hold on to the poverty gospel, we will drag down those around us. We'll come to their doorstep asking for money or food when we really should be working hard to support the work of ministry.

You don't have to be poor to honor Jesus.

Get Your Mind Right about Money

The problem with both false money gospels is that their value lies in the scorecard of money. You have it and you're good, or you don't have it and you're good. Money is the spiritual measuring stick.

Money is not a spiritual measuring stick, though. Proverbs 21:2 says that the Lord weighs the heart. Our heart shows our spiritual condition. The outworking of our heart is faith, and we are measured by faith in Christ as a pass/fail test. It is not the strength of our faith, but the strength of the object of our faith that saves us.

Money is a neutral thing, a store of value. Did you know that in the U.S. our money is not even worth the paper that it is printed on? While every dollar used to be backed by its value in gold, we now have a system called fiat money. Fiat money is an IOU of value established by a government. So money is really just a piece of paper with a promise, like Monopoly money.

It certainly cannot be a unit of salvation.

If we have a twisted theology of money, our work will be a complete mess. We will either be busy accumulating paper IOUs, or we will be puffed up with self-righteousness because we are poor. This is pretty ridiculous in both cases and misses the point of the gospel of Jesus altogether.

For freedom Christ has set us free. Free to work, free to risk, free to be rich or poor, depending on our talents, work ethic, and God's provision. I will say that it's much riskier to be rich than poor, however. Jesus said that over and over again.

Neither the prosperity gospel nor the poverty gospel gets us closer to Jesus. The opposite happens as we focus too much on money. And as a follower of Jesus, if my work does not bring me closer to Jesus, I want to do something else.

If we want to get any work done of true significance, we need to avoid bad theology of money and understand that our work is designed to give God glory. The upshot of giving God glory is that we get joy, which is much deeper and stronger than fleeting happiness.

If you have believed a lie in regards to the prosperity gospel or the poverty gospel, drop your chains and run toward the freedom found in Jesus alone. Working unto money as god is a disaster (prosperity gospel) and working unto poverty as god (the poverty gospel) is too. We need to get our mind right about money—that it is simply a unit of measure and a blessing from God as the result of hard work. A misunderstanding of money is a wall that will make your work a misguided trip to nowhere. But this wall is easy to dismantle.

Work hard and trust in the real Gospel. God promises to provide. The end.

TAKE ACTION

<u>Reflection</u>: What do you think about money? Picture a stack of 100-dollar bills on a table in front of you. What feelings does this elicit? Are you a chaser of money, or do you fall into the guilt trap of thinking we shouldn't have any money? Write this down.

<u>Prayer</u>: Money is a gift from God, whether we have very little or very much. Consider your answers to the question above and ask God (remember, by writing on paper) for a new understanding of money. Ask Him for a more generous heart with your financial resources. Write down your prayer.

<u>Action</u>: Write down the material objects you desire. You know, the things that money could buy if only you had enough. Don't holy-roller this—be honest. Write these down on one side of the page. Now, on the other side of the page, write down next to each of these what you currently have (for example, if you dream of having a Lexus but you drive a Ford Fiesta, on the left side of the page write Lexus and on the right side write Ford Fiesta). After you finish these two columns, first take a look at the left column. What does this show you about yourself and your heart's disposition toward money and consumerism? Now take a look at your right column. What does this show you about God's generosity toward you and His care for you? Write down five evidences of God's generosity.

Chapter 4

WALL 2:
RETHINK ASSUMPTIONS

Whoever isolates himself seeks his own desire;
he breaks out against all sound judgment.
A fool takes no pleasure in understanding,
but only in expressing his opinion.
—Proverbs 18:1-2

We now move on to the second wall we must conquer: *assumptions*. Assumptions affect our perception of the world more than we realize. The curious thing about assumptions is that they hold tremendous power, but we scarcely realize they are there. In our work lives, assumptions are everywhere.

Before moving on, let's define *assumption*. An assumption is an accepted truth that we carry through life to help us make sense of our surroundings. For example, we assume that sharks are dangerous, so we tend to stay away from them. We assume that the stove is hot when it glows red. We assume that the sun will rise tomorrow.

As we grow older, we collect assumptions along the way.

Sometimes we form assumptions by seeing something until it becomes expected. The love of a good parent is like this. A child lavished with love from birth will assume that his parents love him. Other assumptions work their way into our minds without much basis. Take racism, for example. Racism is discrimination based upon ignorance about the race discriminated against. The foundation of racism is often a lack of understanding—and thus a racist world view carries bad assumptions. The assumption that all work is miserable is a conclusion drawn from a myopic perspective. It is illogical to assume that all jobs are bad because yours is a beating.

While bad assumptions lead us astray, good assumptions are helpful. We need to make sure that we do not carry bad assumptions, because assumptions are powerful. We need to pay extra attention to our assumptions because we don't want to, er, *assume* assumptions. We must make sure we hold the right assumptions.

In this chapter we'll explore some common assumptions that form walls between our work and our relationship with God. After each assumption we'll discuss how to use a competing assumption to counteract these misleading truths.

Assumption 1 – Retirement is Heaven

You will not find the concept of retirement in the Bible. At least I can't find it. That does not mean that retirement is unbiblical; it just means we'll have to use something other than direct passages from Scripture to form our understanding of retirement. We can still use the bedrock of Scripture as a base— we just need to extend the lines a little bit.

Rest is biblical. God rested after creating the world and put the rhythm of rest into our lives—the Sabbath. So the rest component of retirement is a good thing. But what about years of rest? With life expectancy on the rise thanks to the blessing of modern medicine and nutrition, we now can expect 20 plus years of life after retirement if we retire in our fifties. 20 years is a long time to rest.

Why did God create (and command) rest? We rest because we are tired from work and we need energy to work again. Rest is a means to an end—to work. Sedentary retirement devoid of meaningful contribution to the world in some respect (art, commerce, mentoring, etc.) is rest without purpose. Rest is also an act of trust. As we rest, we knowingly depend upon God for provision and sustenance.

But wait—you worked your entire life to build up that pension or 401(k) so you could retire. You were up before the sun every day and you stayed late. You worked weekends when you needed to. You earned it. Am I saying you should never retire? No—I am not saying you should not retire. But if we think retirement will be like walking through the pearly gates, we deceive ourselves.

We were made to create, not consume.

Here is what I mean—our culture preaches the value of consumption. We want to buy, watch, drink, and wear more than we want to sell, produce, distill, and weave.

But God—whose image we bear—is a creator God, and He has been busy since the beginning of time, creating and sustaining the world. He has millions of children to care for, all while making sure the waves are the right height in Southern California and the temperature is to His liking in Bangladesh. Now, God is outside of time and He is infinitely powerful, so He isn't running around with His hair on fire. He is just working, creating, sustaining. He doesn't stop except to rest and enjoy; then He starts again.

We are immortal beings on a path to eternity. We will enter the chasm of death and then we'll keep going. If we look at death as final ("you only go around once"), it makes sense to coast for 20 years until we exhale our last breath. But death isn't final. It is transitional. And since death isn't final, retirement is not as important as we've made it. You won't miss out if you retire late or never retire. If you can retire and transition your life into another phase, that's great, but if you can't retire or simply don't want to—that's okay too.

<u>Corrective assumption</u>: *Retirement is another phase of production.*

Consider retirement the beginning of a new phase of creativity, instead of being let out to pasture. If you have lived long enough to reach retirement age, you have sacred wisdom to share. Perhaps you could mentor young folks or finally take up painting. Write a book, build furniture, or consult with businesses.

The key is to leverage wisdom and resources for God's glory and for the benefit of those around us. Keep moving, even if your pace slows. God isn't done with you. Go make something beautiful and don't slip into a consumer mindset just because you're up in years—that'll make your soul wither and rot. Create something—art, gardens, relationships with young people, a new business—and your later years will be filled with adventure, risk, and vibrant experiences. And you'll continue the dance with God by making something of value.

Assumption 2 – Your Work Doesn't Matter

Let me give you a gross example of how all work matters. I once saw a TV show called *Dirty Jobs with Mike Rowe* where a livestock rancher named Albert castrated young lambs. Albert had stumbled upon a new method that was more humane than the old method of tying a rubber band around the testicles of the young animals until the testicles finally died and fell off. The old school method was slow and painful, but Albert's method was quick and caused less pain.

The method Albert had created: make a small incision on the scrotum and then pull the testicles out with your teeth.

Albert's job can bring God as much glory as your favorite pastor. His work matters. If Albert understands that He is not just castrating lambs with his teeth, but rather that He is fulfilling the command laid forth in Genesis 1 to have dominion over the creatures of the earth, he will connect his work to the glory of God. All work (unless nefarious, illegal, or harmful) is legitimate and all work matters.

People have asked me, "What about those people who dig ditches or clean toilets? How can they find fulfillment in their work? Does their work matter?" Of course it does. Same deal with Albert. We need ditches dug so that water drains properly in our communities, and of course we need toilets cleaned. If no one dug ditches, we'd have a mess on our hands, and if no one cleaned toilets, we'd have an even bigger mess—and maybe some sickness associated with the filth. If you focus on the positive contribution of the job, you will start to see hints of God's design in the work.

Corrective assumption: *Your work matters because it is an opportunity to contribute to society and to work hard for God's glory.*

Your current job is an ordained opportunity, not a useless drag. Eternities are at stake for those around you who do not know God—and your influence just might point them to Him. Furthermore, the world needs your contribution. If you connect your labor to God's command to work and be fruitful, you'll see light break through in your job. Seize the opportunity today because tomorrow may not come.

Assumption 3 – You Are Not Creative

I hear it all the time.

"I am not creative."

"I am type A."

"I am left brain."

We like to put ourselves in categories almost as much as we like to categorize others. It helps us reduce the complexity of the human condition into understandable parts. The problem is that people don't fit into categories. When we decide we are not creative, what we are really saying is that even though we bear the image of God—the *imago dei*—some of His image didn't make it into our DNA.

Nonsense.

Now, surely there are people who are more artistic than others, but I believe we all have creativity and art within us as part of our wiring harness. Our Heavenly Father created out of nothing and dreamed up an impossibly complex and beautiful world. He paints each day, a red-orange, bursting sunrise illuminating bright-green, waxy leaves of trees. The smile of a child. The hand of a spouse. God is an artist. He likes to show off. And creating new and beautiful art in the world fits right into this mission.

Theologians say there are communicable attributes and noncommunicable attributes of God in our making as humans. A communicable attribute is an attribute that we share with God and a noncommunicable attribute is an attribute we do not share with God. For example, we have a moral mind. We know what is right and what is wrong. This is a communicable attribute.

Creativity is also a communicable attribute we share with God. You won't put the feathers on an oriole or shape a redwood tree, but you are made to make something. This is why art resonates with us—because through artistic creation we declare the glory of God.

Your creativity might mean you solve a technological problem in the software system of a windmill. It could be using a fresh way to inform young minds at school. Or, in the traditional sense, you might paint or draw or write. Our creative potential is endless. God gives us the capacity to create new things to share His incomprehensible love with others. Creative efforts give other people a glimpse of the beauty of God, just as Paul explains that nature highlights the attributes of God (Rom. 1). Since God's glory is endless and we are small grains of sand (though prized ones in God's eyes) in this whole deal, we cannot over-communicate the majesty of God. It's beyond us. But we can try.

Corrective assumption: *You are creative and must create.*

Not to get all motivational speaker on you, but you have untapped potential in you. A wealth of it. Whether you have bought into the lie that you "just aren't creative" or you know you have a creative bent, the world has not yet seen the end of your creativity. You bear the image of the Consummate Craftsman. Show us what you got.

I once had a conversation with a ferocious woman of God who is a successful writer and speaker. She said something that I will never forget: "You have to find the thing you can't *not do.*" The double negative wasn't a slip of speech—it was her point. When we find the creative outlet that keeps us up at night and grabs our daydreams we have probably found our creative outlet. For me, this is writing. I simply cannot keep myself from sitting down in front of my keyboard and letting my fingers dance words into being. It's addictive for me.

We need to chase down creative outlets in our careers. We may not have creative careers per se, but when you approach your job as a craftsman you will uncover opportunities to breathe your creative design into the work of your hands. I also believe we need to pursue creativity in art as well, even if it's just a hobby. When we paint, draw, write, sing, dance, take photos, or build a sculpture we are letting our creativity out of its cage so that it can flow into the hearts of others. It is habit forming. Maybe for you that's sitting down at the kitchen table and drawing a picture of a goat. If you understand that producing art will open your heart to more of God's beauty and that we need your art to see God more clearly, hopefully that'll be enough to get your hands moving.

We want to see what you create. Go make something.

Assumption 4: You Are Stuck

Years ago I sat in my car outside my office, eating a mediocre sandwich (this isn't a euphemism; I was indeed eating a very average sandwich). I stared straight ahead as I chewed, my mind going anywhere else but always finding a path back to where I was and didn't want to be. I had racked up credit card debt hoping my career in real estate would take off, but it hadn't and hope was lost. I was lost.

I was stuck.

I had studied for this career in college. My job was to support my wife and our future children. I was committed and had no backup plan. But things weren't going the way I had hoped. I guess I should have remembered James 4:

> Come now, you who say, "Today or tomorrow we will go into such and such a town and spend a year there and trade and make a profit"—yet you do not know what tomorrow will bring. What is your life? For you are a mist that appears for a little time and then vanishes.
>
> —James 4:13-14

I thought I'd be making good money within a year, but I was broke. Lindsay and I had plans but life wasn't cooperating with our plans, despite plenty of effort. My plan had failed. It was James 4 in action.

We have a measure of free will, but our free will plays within the bounds of God's grand plan. His plans will stand, not mine and not yours. And that's a really good thing.

God is loving to destroy our plans when needed. If we think we're completely in control, we are in for a rude awakening. Once we know that our lives are not our own and that control is an illusion, we find the freedom of letting go.

Maybe your plans aren't working out. Or maybe you never planned to be where you are—but you feel stuck. You have bills and responsibilities. Maybe your image is tied to your work, but you hate your job. I get it. But you are not stuck. You are free. You must heed your responsibilities and duties, of course. If you are in the military, you are duty bound for a specified time. If you support your family with your income, quitting your job would be selfish and stupid without a means to care for them.

God puts us in our places with loving intention, and we are to play our part as best we can. But our part may change. 1 Corinthians 7:21 instructs us,

Were you a bondservant when called? Do not be concerned about it. (But if you can gain your freedom, avail yourself of the opportunity.)
—1 Corinthians 7:21

If you find yourself in a career that feels like slavery, avail yourself of the opportunity to do something else. If you live in America like I do, you live in a land of opportunity. You are where God wants you to be but that doesn't mean He intends for you to stay there forever.

Corrective assumption: ***You are free to move, but use your head.***

You may have a Jerry Maguire fantasy of leaving your job in a blaze of glory. You may be tempted to tell your boss to take this job and shove it.

Not so fast.

You are not stuck. You can change your career, and maybe you should. But you bear the name of Jesus, and it's possible that the only Jesus your colleagues know is what you show them. When we leave a job it should be with a graciousness and respect—and love. And further, getting unstuck may take some time.

If you feel stuck, you aren't. Go ahead—get up and move. Just let love mark your steps.

Every morning we carry assumptions into the day. If we aren't careful we will bring assumptions that point us in the wrong direction. It will cloud our days instead of sharpening them. If we pay attention, we can take out our assumptions and lay them on the table and sort through them. Keep that one. That's trash. Ooh—that one. When we populate our unconscious minds with the eternal promises of God, our assumptions will shift from disabling to empowering.

So, to review our corrective assumptions:

- Retirement is another phase of production.
- Your work matters because it is an opportunity to work hard for God's glory.
- You are creative and must create.
- You are free to move, but use your head.

Don't accept the status quo of assumptions. Take hold of better ones.

TAKE ACTION

Reflection: How do assumptions guide your life? What assumptions do you need to discard in addition to the ones mentioned in this chapter? Write this down.

Prayer: Our assumptions must be rooted in God's truth. Pray about the assumptions you want to believe and carry with you at work. For example, ask God to show you that you aren't working so you can cash out and move to resort (retirement is heaven), but rather that you are working because work is a blessed command. Ask God for more joy and delight in your daily grind. Write down your prayer.

Action: This will be interactive. Invite a friend or coworker to have coffee (or lunch, or a beer) to discuss work. You can go as deep as you want (it'll depend somewhat on the depth of your partner) but explain your former assumptions and your new understandings. Ask them about their assumptions about work. Encourage them in their work. Write down your experience.

Chapter 5

WALL 3:
ENTITLEMENT

Our next wall is built within your brain. And it is a serious killer of doing work that matters. It can inhibit our relationship with the Lord as well. Let's talk about *entitlement*.

It was a warm afternoon. I left my office in a hurry. Hitting *send* on an email, I hurried to the conference room for our second interview of the day. We were searching for an entry-level team member, and so far we weren't having much luck. As I walked into the conference room, there he sat. His jacket was slung over the back of a chair, and he leaned back in the conference room chair as if it were his living room. He barely said "hello" as I walked in. The keys to his Audi sat on the table in front of him.

Great start.

As we talked, it became obvious he didn't want the job. And it was also apparent he had not read the job description, so I read it to him. I explained the job description again, trying to hide my frustration. He looked at me.

"A monkey could do this job."

"I'm sorry?"

"A monkey could do this job," he repeated.

The interview was over shortly after that. I thanked him through gritted teeth and showed him out. We eventually hired someone for the job (a person, not a monkey).

This stellar interviewee was entitled. He didn't have a job and needed one but was clearly of the opinion that he was above the job he was interviewing for—a job with a great company and plenty of upward mobility. It was okay that he didn't want the job, but the way he went about it was ridiculous.

Entitlement is a self-created wall that smothers our faith from informing our work, and most of us have at least a small amount of entitlement that needs killing. If we walk into situations always expecting to get our due, we'll not only be insufferable, but we will also avoid God-honoring hard work. Entitlement is a form of pride, and pride precedes destruction according to Proverbs 16:18. If you want to connect your work and faith, entitlement must go.

The American Dream

Entitlement has crept into the American Dream. The American Dream was born many years ago in the hearts and minds of hard-working Americans. The goal was a happy family with a house and white fence. Well along with many things in the U.S., the American Dream has morphed and changed into something else. This is not good 'ole days talk or a rant about how we need to go back to the former version of the American Dream. Though this may sound relativistic, I believe the American Dream is subjective and should be defined by each person or each family. That's freedom. But not all American Dreams are equal in the long run. You don't need a *Leave It to Beaver* life to find deep fulfillment—you need Jesus.

The problem: the American Dream now comes with entitlement.

No one owes us anything. We don't bring a scroll of rights into this world based on our birth. What we have defined in the Constitution are the rights that the Founding Fathers believed God hardwires into us all, but we have seen that even the Constitution can be amended or interpreted based on the subjective opinion of man. I am a fan of our Constitution, but it will not save us.

Americans are fed a message that everyone is owed the American Dream, loosely defined as an ever-increasing minimum standard of living. It used to be that we fought for equal rights, but now we fight for equal prosperity. We are told that prosperity is a right and not something that God may or may not grant as the fruit of hard work over time.

I am not being political here. Both left and right have perverted and entitled notions of the American Dream. The point is that entitlement will hinder our work and our faith. Here is how: when we carry entitlement with us to our job, we look through distorted lenses. Instead of humble thankfulness and hard work, we obsess over the end result of our work and whether or not we are getting the money and affirmation we deserve. We make sure we get our due. The work itself now becomes a means to an end. Instead of working as unto the Lord, we are working as unto our version of what we are owed.

This attitude is a major impediment to doing great work.

Here we look to Jesus as our example. Surely He was a good carpenter and worked hard at His craft. He worked with a humble and passionate spirit, sweat and service. The work was valuable because it honored His Dad and served other people. So He worked.

If we feel entitled to a certain level of pay, standard of living, or recognition, we'll walk around with our palms outstretched, while our hands should be clasped in prayer or busy working.

Thankfulness

The antidote to entitlement is thankfulness. The posture of thankfulness is the opposite of entitlement. Thankfulness accepts the way things are—good or bad—and sees the goodness of God in it all.

Consider what Paul tells the Ephesians about thankfulness:

Giving thanks always and for everything to God the Father in the name of our Lord Jesus Christ.

—Ephesians 5:20

Giving thanks *always* and for *everything* to God in the name of Jesus. Now that is hard to do. But what a godly mindset! Let's dig deeper to mine the riches of this verse.

1. <u>Give thanks always</u>. Paul suggests a posture of constant thankfulness. Not only that, but an outwardly gracious attitude. This is hard, to remain thankful when the going gets tough. To give thanks always is to be a delightful and godly person—a person who will work hard with delight.

2. <u>For everything</u>. Everything includes, well, everything. To be thankful for everything means that we find God's grace in all of life and that we are grateful for all of it. This means that even in the dark times of our lives we should remain upwardly thankful to our God who supplies every need of ours according to the riches in glory in Christ (Phil. 4:19). When we are thankful for everything, we have reached a maturity such that we can see the good when the good is hard to see. When you sit in the waiting room of the hospital after the death of a loved one, there is the love of family and friends there to bless you. When you get fired and you have to go home to your

wife and three kids who depend upon you, there is the laughter of your child and a sweet innocence of knowing it'll all work out, Daddy. Thanks to the riches in glory in Jesus—which He bought with His blood—we can be thankful for everything because God doles out grace even in the most unlikely places.

3. <u>To God the Father in the name of our Lord Jesus Christ</u>. Mere thankfulness isn't much help if we have no one to thank. Our sovereign God is the source of all love, all goodness. In our constant thankfulness, we look to Him as the One to whom we should be thankful. But we must specifically understand the value of the gospel of Jesus Christ at the altar of thankfulness. The gospel—what Jesus did on the cross—changes our hearts made of rock into beating hearts of flesh. Hearts that can love God and hearts that can be thankful. So we are thankful for the gospel and also thankful because of the gospel. The cross allows us to be thankful. As the blood ran down the worn planks of the cross, Jesus broke down the dividing wall of hostility which sin built between us and the Father. Thus, we are able to say thank you.

Thankfulness is the lifeblood of a healthy work life.

The Wrong Story

My faith became a part of my work when I began to realize that I had been looking at the story of my life from the wrong perspective. Though I never meant it to be, life was *The Truman Show*, an experience where I was me and the rest of the world was not me—but somehow I was the center of it all. Life was about my financial gain, my righteous image, and my pursuit of pleasure. I obsessed over trying to make money early in my career in commercial real estate and missed huge opportunities to serve others in my work. This is the wrong story. It is not only illogical and megalomaniacal, but it is a story of entitlement.

Many of us still live inside that story.

It all clicks when we start to realize that life and work aren't about us. Work that is devoted to others—God, your family, your friends, strangers, society—is a blessed endeavor. It's a worthy mission. And yes, there is something in it for us. That is okay. But the joy that we receive is a byproduct of first fighting for the joy of others.

If you are an insurance agent and all you care about is building your kingdom, you'll sell people whatever they will buy, and you will pressure people until they stop taking your calls. On the other hand, if you are focused on serving others and making sure that in the event of a disaster they are covered financially by proper insurance, you will not only derive great joy from helping others, but you also shouldn't be surprised to find that other people are interested in working with you. (It's almost like God designed it that way.)

Work intended to serve others is good work. It resonates with others and it's attractive. Stepping outside the skin of self-consciousness, we can take big risks and put ourselves out there for the good of other people. We can see ourselves only if we stand still in front of a mirror, and an others-focused approach leaves no time for that nonsense. Don't stand still—get moving and get away from the mirror. It's not about you.

When entitlement becomes a navel-gazing party, we will pour out our piggy banks over and over just to count the money and keep score. We'll check our email and social media constantly to see who cares about what we are doing. Our time will be devoted to checking our position with others—are we winning? Are we getting our due? And time spent on endless self-evaluation is time not spent doing.

An outward focus is the ticket. What do other people really

need? What do they want? How can I leverage my strengths and opportunities to create something of value to them?

If you have read (and liked) *Atlas Shrugged*, you are at this point ready to burn this book and jump on a plane and fly to a secret hideaway place where people like me don't exist. In *Atlas*, Ayn Rand shows through a fictional story how spineless and fake others-centeredness can ruin an economy. As the book progresses, any talk of helping other people for their own good becomes heresy because of the distortion caused by fake altruists.

Though I think Rand was an atheist and we may not see eye-to-eye on some things, I get her point. The point is that to live a fake story of helping "the common good" by leeching off others is an abomination. It ruins cultures and drags down those doing great work. Devote yourself to creating work that is so good that others benefit and even desire to be a part of what you are doing. Call it altruistic capitalism.

And (gasp!) people should pay you for your work. If what you produce has no monetary value whatsoever, it might well be that other people aren't blessed enough by it to pay for it. We vote with our dollars. The Bible says that a laborer deserves wages. Payment is not antithetical to loving other people, especially if you use a portion of your money to further glorify God by loving others deeply. We need God's blessings to flow through our fingers, not rot in our fists.

We are caught up in a story much bigger than us. We did not write it and we aren't the protagonist. The Writer allows us to play a part. But this Writer is no ordinary writer, making his characters writhe in pain for the reader's pleasure. No, the fundamental difference between God as a writer and John Steinbeck is that God writes from a place of benevolent holiness. God has always lacked nothing—so He writes out of abundance. As characters in His story we will, like it or not, be subject to the desires of the Writer. What I mean is that if God were a big, angry God throwing lightning bolts at scared children, we should probably cower in a cave. But God's heart is love. He enjoys Himself by lavishing us with love as we look up at Him and smile like a kid just given a cherry Popsicle.

But what about the Old Testament? God seems pretty Zeus-like there. A ton of people have died gruesome deaths through wars and plagues and what not—and God was not standing by that river helpless as they drowned. He even brought the flood.

Well, the thing is, God's story is pretty complicated. I'm not about to write words that make it all make sense to you, either. But when you look at the big picture, you see that every event has God's purpose weaved into it. And God is perfect so His purpose is perfect. So if we find ourselves breathing water in a raging river, we can still trust Him. I have heard it said this way: if we knew what God knows, we'd play it the exact same way.

Live the right story. Look to others and try to meet their needs in the marketplace.

The Will of God Should Prosper In Our Hands

The will of the Lord shall prosper in his hand.
—Isaiah 53:10

Throughout Isaiah, we see clear foreshadowing about Jesus. The verse above is referring to Jesus—that the will of the Lord prospered in His hand. This verse is alluding to Jesus' crucifixion, so one can gather that the will of the Lord prospered in Jesus' nail-pierced, bloody hands. It was an exceedingly painful thing for the will of God to prosper in Jesus' hands.

This idea—the will of God prospering in our hands—is worth exploring.

First, we won't always see the will of God prospering in our hands, even if it is. One thing I have learned through years of eldership of a local church is that you don't get to see the work of your hands completely. The seeds we sow often grow outside our field of view, but many grow into great oaks. God weaves small stories into His grand story, and we are just subplots, though important ones. If the will of God prospers in our hands, it's because His hands are moving through ours.

Second, we should seek to make the will of God prosper in our hands through our work. God will carry out His will with us or without us, but He invites us to play. We can play a part. The Bible tells us if we follow Jesus, the part we play is marked with love, so we can start and end with love. Your work should be marked by love, whether you're a lawyer or a potter.

Finally, it might get messy. Historically, when God's will prospers through someone it's rough on them. Standing in the stream of the Almighty can leave our bodies broken and bruised. Sure, God might well use a successful new business venture to prosper His will in your hands. He might have you create beautiful music for others to enjoy. But it'll wear you out if you're doing it right. (When you're exhausted or beaten down just remember to head back to the well of life and sit at Jesus' feet.)

Seeking the will of God at work is a dagger in the heart of entitlement. If we live for His story, our story will start to mean something again, and we won't have to check our stats. Entitlement robs us of the deep joy of living for another, but the good news is that through thankfulness, living in the right story, and seeking to do God's will in our work, we can crush the wall of entitlement.

The gospel has no room for entitlement. As my friend and pastor Scott says, we are not merely "undeserving" of the grace of Jesus; we are "ill-deserving." If we orient ourselves around the fact that we are sinners in need of a Savior who lavishes favor based upon no merit of our own, it'll be hard to hang on to entitlement.

We become what we behold. The more we behold Jesus, the more we'll be made like Him—and Jesus and entitlement don't hang out in the same place.

TAKE ACTION

Reflection: We are all entitled to some degree. To what do you feel entitled? Where do you believe you aren't getting your due? Write this down.

Prayer: Great work has no room for entitlement. God's work has no room for entitlement. Ask God to kill your entitlement and to show you that while you are owed nothing, He has blessed you lavishly. Write down this prayer.

Action: Write this down: "Work is a means to honor God and to enjoy Him in action." I'm serious, write it down. Now read this and think about how different it is to work for the sake of the work (to God's glory) instead of working to get what we're owed. Consider the freedom this provides.

Chapter 6

WALL 4:
CULTURE WARS

Okay, so we have tackled the walls of our perspective on money, assumptions, and entitlement. We are making good progress. These walls are internal walls that live within our mind. But the outside world also creates walls that make it tough to bring our faith and work together. Let's now move to the wall of *culture*.

What will you do when your faith in Jesus collides cultural norms? What if exercising your faith at work becomes illegal? Are you prepared for this?

As I write this, the dust is still settling on the Supreme Court ruling that gay marriage is a constitutional right. Bruce (Caitlyn) Jenner, a former Olympian, was just awarded the Arthur Ashe Courage Award at the ESPY awards for his (her) sex-change transformation. Technology grows and morphs at an unprecedented speed. Text messages replace phone calls and social media replaces text messages. Busyness is a badge of honor and people are more distracted than ever—historically speaking.

Times are a-changing.

People have said this forever. Each generation sits on the porch and bemoans the next one. Ecclesiastes says there's nothing new under the sun. Well, yes, of course. That's in the Bible so it's true. But old issues manifest themselves in new ways. The culture in the United States is indeed changing, and what with social media and the internet, it is changing at warp speed. The cultural standards of morality are hard to pin down—as they move constantly. Some will call this advancement of the human race, or evolution. I wouldn't and here is why: in order to know if you are making headway you have to know where you are headed. And since our society has no rudder and no unified goal, I can't see how we can draw a straight line from here to anywhere. I don't mean to be a downer, but wherever we are headed I'm pretty sure the trajectory isn't toward Jesus.

Some say the faith of the Founding Fathers of the U.S. was deism at best—a vague notion of God with an agnostic lean. Others will push back on that and claim that we were founded as a Christian nation. I wasn't there with them in the dank air of Independence Hall as they drew the shades and crowded around the Constitution. I have toured Independence Hall, and as I stood there I pictured a room full of brilliant men of various faiths, all sweating together in their goofy clothes, trying to form a nation out of nothing. These men brought their predispositions into the room with them, and as they talked their diverse views swirled around into the document of the Constitution.

But religious faith in general was held in high regard. No doubt about that.

The First Amendment protects the country from an establishment of a national religion and also ensures the free exercise of religion by individuals. The Declaration of Independence was written with the assumption of a capital "C" Creator, which endows certain rights to us. Whether we were founded as a specifically Christian nation or not, the U.S. was founded by men who held faith in high regard, and most of them believed in God.

It is not logical—or fair—to say that the gay marriage ruling is an example that this country no longer cares about faith. That's a wild overreaction. But this ruling is indicative that the cultural tide of America is changing (or has already changed). And it has changed based on a new paradigm: a relativism (i.e. what's true for me may not be true for you—truth is relative). Whereas many great thinkers of old searched for truth and let the truth shape them, relativism says we mold truth to fit our preferences.

According to a Pew Research Center study, between the years of 2007 and 2014 those "unaffiliated" with religion jumped from 16.1 percent to 22.8 percent. That's a big change in seven years. Those claiming "Non-Christian Faiths" rose from 4.7 percent to 5.9 percent. "Evangelical Protestant" dropped from 26.3 percent to 25.4 percent.[6] Looking at the data from the Greatest Generation (those who came up during the Great Depression) chronologically to the Millennial generation, the percentage of those claiming Christian faith declines sharply with each generation.

This probably doesn't surprise you. Whereas before it was okay to assert that there was a God in general, it takes more courage now to assert your belief that God exists at all.

No Real Change?

So what do we do about it? March at the courthouse? Put more fish stickers on our bumper (not the kind with legs—I'm not too bright but I think that's a subtle insult to Christians)? Maybe we should go on tirades on social media? Some of you have taken the louder route.

The louder route is not winsome in most cases. There is a time to protest and throw down, but when it comes to engaging a culture that is swimming in the opposite direction of us spiritually, shouting is a bit like throwing an egg at a car. You might make someone mad, but you surely won't change where they are headed.

The statistics and trends are a little alarming. Certainly they aren't feel-good stats. As a Christian it is not a positive thing to watch people turn away from professed faith in Christ. But what if the crowd was just hushed by social norms before? Perhaps there were many in the crowd who asserted faith in Jesus only because that's what was commonly accepted. Here in the Bible Belt, there is a segment of the older population who are not Christians but went to church on Sunday because that's what you did. You went to church and then you had lunch. In contrast to the "pot roast after church" generation, we are moving into a time when asserting faith in Jesus will cost something—which, by the way, is the historical norm for following Jesus.

The polls and surveys portray an overly pessimistic outcome which, while true in regards to the trend of culture, is skewed by this phenomenon of church culture evaporating. Put simply, it looks worse than it is—but the tide is moving out from the shore of Christianity.

In his *Christianity Today* article entitled "Farewell, Cultural Christianity," Russell D. Moore explains,

> *As American culture secularizes, the most basic Christian tenets seem ever more detached from mainstream American culture. There is, for those who came and will come of age in recent years, no social utility in embracing them. Those who identify with Christianity, and who gather with the people of God, have already decided to walk out of step with the culture. These Christians have already embraced strangeness by spending Sunday morning at church rather than at brunch.*[7]

Because Christian faith is—or will soon become—culturally scandalous, those who claim to follow Jesus do so at the expense of their reputation. Expressing your faith may hinder your career advancement. As Mr. Moore says in his article, there is longer any real "social utility" in following Jesus. As pastor Matt Chandler says, being a Christian at the office won't make you the cool guy. No, we will be weirdos—and increasingly so. Because no one wants to be an anathema, this smokes out nominal Christians.

At least people are getting real with what they actually believe.

So are we seeing real, meaningful change? Is this a cultural shift or just a tide change, like a financial market correction? I believe we are seeing a real cultural shift. A cultural shift is a long-term, penetrating change while a tide change is just like the tide—in and out it goes, until it goes in and out again. God changes the course of history as He wishes, so in no way am I suggesting here that we are on a dead end road to hell with nowhere to u-turn. But yes, we are seeing real change in our culture in America which will affect followers of Jesus in their work lives. We will be put in positions where we will take a stand for what we believe, or we will cower.

Working in Exile

It's not just that there is a separation between the state and religion, which is mandated by law. There is also a separation between work and faith. The separation between work and faith is not legislated for the most part, but walk into most work environments and start talking about your faith in Jesus and people will look at you like you have two heads. I noticed this phenomenon when I entered the business world, that the socially-acceptable thing to do is to keep your faith stuffed down into your briefcase so everyone could get their work done and "religion" could be kept private.

Religion is a protected class under the Civil Rights Act of 1964. The intent of the law is to reduce discrimination based upon religion. This means that you cannot ask a job candidate about their religious beliefs. You cannot ask this because it would be possible to discriminate if a company (or individual) chose to hire only people of a certain religion or to outlaw hiring people of a certain religion. The idea is that if you don't know what people believe, you cannot treat them unfairly based on their beliefs. And this seems to be the initial intent—to make sure people do not discriminate against others with competing religious views.

But an unintended consequence of making religion a protected class is that it makes us scared to talk about our faith at work. What can we say legally? What is professional? *Maybe it's best I just keep this to myself.* We feel pressured to shut our faith out of our work. Combine this element with the decline in social utility of being a Christian and there is a very strong temptation to remain silent as a church mouse at work.

But remaining quiet is not an option. Because Christian views will smash against the rocks of the views of the majority, those of us who follow Jesus will be put to the test. We need to be prepared.

We must remember, however, that in most situations we aren't being paid to evangelize our coworkers. We are hired to do a job, whether that's designing video games or selling lumber. If we spend our time trying to convert everyone around us, not only will we not be winsome, but we will avoid doing the very job for which we were hired. This is not the right approach. The right approach is to perform with excellence and to be ready to share the reason for the hope that is in you.

Burwell v. Hobby Lobby Stores, Inc. reveals what happens when freedom of religion creates a situation where a choice must be made as to whose religion gets to be freely exercised. What happened in this case was that Hobby Lobby objected to the mandate by the Affordable Care Act ("Obamacare") to pay for insurance coverage for employees which includes certain "emergency" contraceptives. Hobby Lobby believed that some of these contraceptives induced early abortions and thus, based upon the Christian faith of the owners of Hobby Lobby, they objected and filed a lawsuit. The Supreme Court ruled in favor of Hobby Lobby, thus setting a strong precedent. But as author and *The Gospel Coalition* columnist Trevin Wax put it in his article shortly after the decision, "You may be thrilled at the Hobby Lobby verdict, but there's a good chance your neighbor isn't."[8] Misinformation, outrage, and tirades followed the decision like a swarm of wasps.

Here is the tension: per Romans 13, we should be subject to the governing authorities that God has put in place, while in Matthew 10:32 Jesus tells us that we should acknowledge Him before men. What if the authorities put laws into place that make it illegal to acknowledge Jesus before others? The question brings us to a crucial juncture—the point at which integrating our faith into work creates conflict between the law of the land and biblical Christianity. For example, will a Christian baker be legally required to make wedding cakes for same sex couples if the baker objects on biblical grounds? Will a Christian contractor be required to build a satanic temple, or is declining the work discrimination based on freedom of religion? Will companies be permitted to object to legislation that they believe tramples on their faith?

In *Hobby Lobby*, the answer was yes—a company can object to legislation that conflicts with the religious views of its owners or employees. But many other dilemmas will arise that will test the limits of religious freedom as it relates to Christianity.

Christians will win some and lose some.

So what will you do when faced with a dilemma between your faith in Jesus and your career? What will you do if your faith makes you a criminal? I pray you choose Jesus. Jesus was crucified for making the true assertion that He was God. The apostles were jailed and slaughtered. Christians throughout history have wet the blades of their persecutors' swords with their blood. And it was worth it. The truth is the truth, and unless you don't really believe, there's no choice but to choose affirming our faith.

We must stand firm in our convictions while remaining humble and gracious. We will be tested, and we must show a loving resolve that is otherworldly.

Engage Culture in Love

As culture stratifies spiritually, we'll find that our workplace is a great big mission field. We rub shoulders with believers and unbelievers of all stripes in the course of our work, so we need to know how to engage them. Remember, a mission field is a place to soak the ground with your sweat and blood through acts of service to others. And because we spend 8 hours a day for 50 weeks for 40 years in the workplace, we're in the field a lot.

I do not advocate obnoxious expression of Christian faith in the workplace (or anywhere, for that matter). A dogmatic, intrusive, and over-the-top expression of faith in Jesus would be contrary to the nature of Jesus Himself. But we must be willing to step into the fray and risk our reputation for the sake of the renown of Jesus. It's not that He needs us to run His PR campaign, but as God's children we carry a family name.

Let's talk about how we should carry ourselves.

Be Brave and Humble. We should be brave and humble in our workplace. We should be eager to help, inclined to listen, and always willing to stand up for what is right. We should be ready to stand up for others. Now this doesn't mean we become defensive and it certainly doesn't mean we walk around with a chip on our shoulder—but sometimes we must look someone in the eye and level with them. Jesus' ministry was humble yet strong. One moment He is whipping dudes out of the temple and the next He is washing someone's feet. Scripture inspires us to courageous, confident love. So it goes with our work. Our work should be soaked in courage and love.

Speak Clearly. In all matters of our career we should speak clearly and let our *yes* be *yes* and our *no* be *no* (Matthew 5:37). Our word must mean something. This is why it's important that we favor listening over talking (James 1:19) and that we always think before speaking. If our word means something and the reputation of Jesus is at stake here, we don't want to go around with loose lips. Measure your words, use them tactfully, but for God's sake, use them.

Use Gentle Bluntness. Jesus was blunt at times too, calling people broods of vipers and making it clear that some people were headed for hell. Not exactly tame watercooler talk. The most effective leaders I have had the pleasure to work with were gently blunt. They would speak the truth clearly, even when it stung someone's feelings. We must favor truth over feelings, while at the same time showing utmost respect for those around us. A word spoken in private most always beats a public declaration when someone's reputation is at stake.

Ultimately, our action plan is quite simple—regardless of where culture goes. We should heed Jesus' words in John 13:35 and mark ourselves by love with everything we do. I have heard it said that the opposite of love isn't hate—it's indifference. We cannot work with indifference toward those eternal souls around us.

Are you scared to engage your workplace with your faith? Are you afraid of the direction culture is heading? Good. That means you care. Place your faith in God and place your feet on the ground—and go share the light of Christ with your workplace. You might be the only glimpse of Jesus they will ever see.

The sentiment of the culture in which we live can be a wall, but it doesn't have to be. You see, the culture in which we live in the U.S. is weird historically. Throughout history, there weren't many periods of white picket fence Christianity. More like people impaled on fence posts. Christians are still beheaded and discriminated against in various parts of the world, but America has been safe. We won't regress into some sort of barbarism of the past, I don't think. But our "evolution" as a culture will put us in rare situations.

It's easy to get stuck in the weeds about this issue. Watch mainstream news long enough (the leftist news or the rightist news—they both propagandize plenty) and you might check yourself into a facility with padded walls. We need to pay attention, but be careful about what you take into your brain and heart. Check your sources—and measure it all by Scripture.

Take a stand and don't fear reprisal or scorn. But the mission must be love. We must share in love because of love. Not some vague notion of love without roots, but the source of love Himself. Sharing love because of love means dropping our dogma to embrace. Or transforming an argument into an opportunity to get to know someone who disagrees with us and hear them out. God doesn't need us to be His chief of staff.

Jesus dealt with this issue to a blood-spilling degree. How did He react? Let's look.

And as Jesus reclined at table in the house, behold, many tax collectors and sinners came and were reclining with Jesus and his disciples. And when the Pharisees saw this, they said to his disciples, "Why does your teacher eat with tax collectors and sinners?" But when he heard it, he said, "Those who are well have no need of a physician, but those who are sick. Go and learn what this means, 'I desire mercy, and not sacrifice.' For I came not to call the righteous, but sinners."

—Matthew 9:10-13

The tax collectors and sinners with whom Jesus ate were the outcasts, the enemies of society. Some might have even been His enemies. Now, notice Jesus didn't schedule a town hall meeting to dismantle their arguments—He "reclined at table." This phrase is one of my favorite phrases in the Bible. Every time we see Jesus "recline at table," He is breaking bread with people and spending time with them because He loves them and desires their company. No bait and switch—just good wine and laughter with heavy helpings of loving truth.

Engage culture in love. Stand firm in your faith. Trials will come, but the joy granted by the grace of Christ withstands all.

TAKE ACTION

Reflection: How does the pressure of culture influence your faith in general? Are you scared to share your views when they are controversial? What situations make you want to keep your faith in Jesus to yourself? Write this down.

Prayer: Pray for your city, your state, and your country. Ask God how your work could influence the culture to see Him in a beautiful light, even if subtly. Write down your prayer.

Action: Today you will influence others, and they will influence you. Resolve today to show the love of Christ in your work. Write down one step—just one—that you could take to better reflect Jesus to the world in your work. Now do that one thing.

Chapter 7

WALL 5:
KILLING PERFECTIONISM

You therefore must be perfect, as your heavenly Father is perfect.

—*Matthew 5:48*

W e now move to our fifth wall. And this one is a little sneaky. It sounds like valiant effort, but it encourages us to fear and fail. I am talking about *perfectionism.* In Matthew 5:48, Jesus tells us we must be perfect. He even goes further than that—He says we have to be perfect as God is perfect. What does Jesus mean here? We know that perfection is unattainable, especially in the context of Matthew 5:43-48, which talks about loving our enemies. Loving even your family is hard, let alone loving those whom you'd consider an enemy. Is Jesus commanding impossible perfectionism? No. We obtain our righteousness through the blood of Christ *because we cannot measure up* to the standard of perfection. Our salvation in Christ is built upon the rubble of our imperfection.

Perfectionism is common for high achievers, especially in the workplace. Many of us think perfectionism is a good thing, and when we say we are a perfectionist we think we're saying something positive—but we aren't. You see, perfectionism puts us back under the unendurable light of the Law. If we are perfectionists, as we death grip every email, every conversation, every report, every ditch dug, we tie our hands together as we beg for failure and disappointment. Because perfect exists only in the life of Jesus.

Can you imagine living under the Old Testament law? Do this, not this. Eat this, not this. Wait—you can't go in there just yet, you need to wear different clothes. Oh yeah—and if you can keep all of God's commandments perfectly, don't get puffed up with pride.

It must have been exhausting to remember all the rules and perform all the rituals. There was a lot to remember and the stakes of failure were high. Jews still live under the burden today, as they do not believe Jesus is the promised Messiah. No Messiah, no freedom from the law. You see, this is fundamental to Christianity, and this is what makes Christianity different from other religions. Other religions (Buddhism, Hinduism, Islam, Judaism) demand divine human performance to move up the ladder spiritually. Placate the gods with your good behavior, and you'll prosper spiritually. Atheists put themselves on the judge stand and then judge themselves by the standard they select—a code of honor or whatever feels good. Again, the key is their performance.

The problem is that we cannot withstand such scrutiny. We are not perfect, and the only perfection we'll ever taste is the imputed righteousness of Christ. *And that's all the perfection we need.*

God didn't create a race of superheroes. He could have, but instead He created complicated bipedal creatures like us. It brings God delight to breathe glory into funny beings. I once saw a stunning piece of art by two artists named Tim Noble and Sue

Webster. If you were to walk into a room with all the lights on and look at their work—sculptures made of scrap metal—you'd think you were looking at either a pile of junk or an abstract art exhibit. But when the right light is turned on, a light which shines light through the junk toward the wall behind the piles, magic happens. Life-like human profiles emerge on shadows on the wall. Light turns the piles of scrap into something beautiful, something unexpected.

Now perhaps this sounds a bit derogatory. We aren't piles of junk. But we are messy for sure, and God does shine His light through our broken forms to bring to light our true humanity. The *imago dei*—the image of God imprinted upon us—is our light.

God rescues us not when we stand atop the mountain of holiness, but when we are dead in our trespasses:

> *But God, being rich in mercy, because of the great love with which he loved us, even when we were dead in our trespasses, made us alive together with Christ—by grace you have been saved—and raised us up with him and seated us with him in the heavenly places in Christ Jesus, so that in the coming ages he might show the immeasurable riches of his grace in kindness toward us in Christ Jesus.*
> —*Ephesians 2:4-7*

Jesus came to fulfill the Law and to free us from the Law at the same time. He came to bring forgiveness for impossibly guilty and flawed people like you and me. His rescue mission was a unilateral move to flood the world with His scandalous love.

That's grace.

We deserved a fiery trial, but got forgiveness as Jesus stood in our place. We could not live perfect lives, so Jesus did that for us. We deserved wrath, so His shoulders bore the weight of the sin of the world as He was mocked and tortured to death.

When you picture the heinous murder of Jesus on the cross, remember He's there in your place. That's our bill of pain He paid. We should be up there.

So why do we still try to be perfect?

If such a price was paid for our perfection by God Himself, how ridiculous of us to think we still have hope of perfection on our own. When we choose to live under the yoke of slavery (the law), we demean Jesus' work on the cross and act as if it didn't happen. *Yeah, I know you paid it all but I'll just clean myself up and do better next time.* The problem is you won't—not if you think you'll just do better under your own power. You may white knuckle good behavior for a little while, but eventually your dark heart will bring forth dark behaviors.

Picture someone in the hospital with two broken legs. They are laid up in bed with Jell-O and ice chips. Let's say they got hit by a truck and both femurs are shattered. Now they could possibly get up and walk under their own power to some extent, but they'll scream in pain and walk crooked and get nowhere fast. They need a doctor to set the bone and put on a cast and get the healing process going. So it goes with us and our perfection. If we demand perfection of ourselves, we'll walk on two broken legs. We need more than a doctor—we need a savior. But if we submit to the grace offered by Jesus, we will heal and go farther than we ever thought possible.

Perfectionism is a wall that emanates from our idol-producing souls. Without contentment in who we are and what we have, we will fall into this snare and start framing up this wall at work. It's not that Jesus can't get through the wall of perfectionism—of course He can, but that those of us who build this wall don't want Him around. We don't trust Him enough to let perfect slip through our fingers. We doubt seriously that God will come through on His promises to fulfill and provide, or that He already has.

We've got to kill perfect.

Perfectionism vs. Excellence

Perfectionism and excellence seem like cousins, but they aren't related at all. In fact, perfectionism and excellence are polar opposites, save the common thread of hard work.

Excellence is hard work in its purest form, a practitioner learning his craft and sweating to perfect it. A perfectionist, on the other hand, is scared. He cannot trust God to provide the increase; he must perform perfectly or else. Mistakes are unacceptable, which makes acquiring wisdom impossible because we learn through mistakes. The perfectionist brings a fearful angst into every task and while he works hard, he tends to miss the forest for the trees. Perfectionism fears imperfection, which is the state in which we imperfect people live.

For many years I held myself and others to a perfect standard of behavior. This was in the name of professionalism. Write a sloppy email or forget to call me back, and I would put a mark in your file in my head. I had a file for myself too. This led to an obsession with responsiveness and people-pleasing, which did produce great service to our company's clients. Deadlines were kept, and the deals I helped them negotiate tended to be very good.

But I was a hungry dog.

When my dog Charlie is hungry, he is obnoxious. He puts his little stick paws on my leg and looks at me with this pleading face that would make you think he hasn't eaten in weeks. But Charlie is a fat and happy little dog, plenty fed and content in every imaginable way.

Hungry yet full.

The dogs have a mighty appetite; they never have enough.
—Isaiah 56:11

Isaiah wasn't talking about Charlie; he was talking about Israel's leaders who lacked wisdom, went after their own interests, and if you go on reading they apparently chugged wine and pontificated on how great tomorrow would be. These guys were like Charlie, hungry yet full—going mad by their unfulfilled desires. Like a perfectionist.

The greatest tyranny of the human soul is to think we are missing out and that God is holding out on us. This lie is what got Adam and Eve to turn on God. We think this little box that God made for us is too small, and if we only broke free there would be exuberance, but we don't realize that we aren't in a box at all. We are free to flourish and move and work fearlessly, but we tend to think we're detained. A perfectionist, trusting in himself, believes the lie that God is holding out. *Perfection must be attained by me because God sure isn't doing His part.*

Excellence in a Christian sense is grace-powered. We don't work to please God or others; we work because Jesus paid our due, and thus we are free. As adopted sons and daughters, we are playing with house money. We are kids at recess. Jesus was perfect, and we get to take on His perfect righteousness like a coat, and from there we push off to work to produce things. The most beautiful art is created through empowered freedmen, those people who understand they can fight for beauty without demanding perfection. Sometimes a slight imperfection, something a little askew, is the capper to great art.

God has always existed in perfect community with Himself in the Trinity: the Father, the Son, and the Holy Spirit. He did not create because He lacked, but the opposite. God created out of abundance. Out of the abundance of His heart He spoke us into being. That's excellence, a love-rooted work ethic to share value with others.

Perfectionism is Highway Robbery

Aim small, miss small. When you aim at something—whether you are shooting a rifle or making a goal—you want to aim at an exact point. Aiming small is the difference between "I am going to build a business this year" and "I am going to open a bakery which will open this year, and it will break even." That's specific and measurable. It should be achievable. That's good goal-making.

But perfectionism will add more parameters to your goals. The standard will never be high enough. The execution of the goals must be spot-on.

But imperfect people execute imperfectly. We have to give ourselves a break. If despite diligence and full effort we do not reach perfection at something, we must release ourselves from the bondage of our unrealistic expectations.

I am a recovering perfectionist. I am not perfect at not being a perfectionist. I get it. When you care about something (a project, a new business, a client relationship), it is tempting to death grip your efforts and ratchet up standards. High standards are great, but an ever-increasing list of standards makes a person go crazy with disappointment. We put on handcuffs of our own making.

Here is how perfectionism harms you:

1. Perfectionism robs the joy of the process. Work is a journey, not a destination. God meets us on the road of work and infuses His presence in our hustle. Perfectionism is a lack of trust in God to handle the outcome of our labor, so we become like the kid trying to climb a tree with a helmet, knee pads, elbow pads, a chest protector, and shoulder pads. It's hard to move like that. Perfectionism screams at us to be careful, and being careful produces nothing of meaning.

2. Perfectionism hurts relationships. Perfectionists are hard to be around. The standards they enforce somehow get forced upon us without our asking. And because as humans we like to project our weaknesses on others (*she is insecure, he's overbearing, etc.*),

perfectionists will transfer some of their unrest to those around them.

3. <u>Perfectionism pickpockets peace</u>. We were designed to work and we were designed to rest. The right measure of these two creates peace and production—an equilibrium of harmony. But perfectionism makes rest a time to freak out about what isn't getting done. (I battle this unrest during times of rest. My head screams to get stuff done while God says to sit still.)

Looking at the great men and women in history whom God used in a big way, we see a laundry list of imperfections. David. Abraham. Paul. Jesus was the only perfect human to ever live, and so He gets to be the only successful perfectionist. If you don't meet Jesus' perfect reputation—which you don't—move on from perfectionism. Now let's talk about where you should move to.

A Better Way: Grace-Driven Hustle

Let's not get out of balance here. Killing perfectionism in no way mitigates effort and high standards—it redeems them. We need to set the bar high in our work and try like crazy to execute the work God has put in our paths. God-sized work demands all of us. I find that when I do something of meaning (like writing this book), I use every ounce of my energy and creativity. During the process of writing I even got a little run down physically and needed to get squared away with exercise and rest. So hard work and hustle is vital to the life of the Christian. (And remember, it'll cost you. You will be tired.)

Take Paul. Paul worked hard at whatever he did. Before he was converted on the road to Damascus, Paul worked hard at persecuting Christians. After he met Jesus, Paul worked hard planting churches and preaching. He also worked hard at his day job, which was building tents.

Paul explains,

But by the grace of God I am what I am, and his grace toward me was not in vain. On the contrary, I worked harder than any of them, though it was not I, but that grace of God that was with me.

—*1 Corinthians 15:10*

Paul hustled so he wouldn't have to depend on the support of others. We don't know exactly what schedule Paul kept, but it is reasonable to assume Paul worked many hours each day on tent-making and preaching. And I love what Paul says about his hard work—that he worked harder than those he was around and that he was driven by God's grace. Not selfish ambition. Not fear of failure. Grace-driven hustle.

When Paul met Jesus on the road to Damascus, he was reborn from the inside out. One moment a persecutor of the church, the next a man on fire to tell the good news of what Jesus had done for him. Paul was blind for three days after meeting Jesus and didn't eat or drink anything. He was blown away.

Grace powers us. We push off from that point of spiritual prosperity to share abundance. We don't work to earn salvation, we work from the point of salvation. Salvation in Christ is a gift, not a goal.

Grace-driven hustle is hard work for the right reasons with the ability to hit the pillow in peace. When we work from the base camp of forgiveness in Christ, we carry with us more love, grace, and peace than we were meant to hold. The excess is supposed to be given away. And we'll need to work hard to make that happen. A churchy-faced Christian who doesn't hustle at work is an abomination—and I have met plenty of them. The hard-working follower of Jesus shows honor and character, while the sluggard brings shame to the family name. If you don't know where to start in your career, just start by working hard.

We are compelled by God's great love to live out our design to work with hustle.

Letting Go and Letting God

The older I get, the more I realize that many cheesy sayings are true. You have probably heard "let go and let God." I like that saying, and I believe it can help us here.

Grace kills perfectionism, not excellence. And when we work hard with trust in God, our work will not only mean something but it will also be *pleasurable*. When we let go of a standard only Jesus Himself could measure up to, we put wind in our sails. We start to run hard like a kid in a playground (perfectionists are more like cats near water).

Work was designed to be pleasurable, even though we now face the thorns and thistles version of work because of the curse of sin. But even with the curse on work, we should still be able to find joy in fulfilling our purpose to work. If you are always miserable, something is wrong. Work is designed to bring great pleasure to you, the worker, and to God, your ultimate employer. There is no reason why we need to dread Mondays and elevate Saturdays. Each day is a gift, and work is a necessary component of our joy.

We spend a ton of time at work in our lifetime. Our work shapes us. If you do forty years of joyful work, the lines on your face will tell others you've smiled a lot. Your valuable contribution will show the world that God is huge and mighty. And I can assure you that your relationships will be much healthier.

If you want to let go and let God, you will first have to come to grips with how small you are. You don't carry the world on your shoulders. You must release your prideful heroism into the arms of Jesus. Next, work hard at whatever you do. When I was growing up, my dad told me "anything worth doing is worth doing well"—that's a good guiding light. Finally, trust God to provide the results, if any.

Grace and perfectionism do not live in the same house. They cannot hang out together. If you embrace grace, you are by nature killing perfectionism—because to receive grace you must accept the fact that grace needs to cover something. What grace covers is our sin, our imperfection. If we think we are without sin we deceive ourselves, and we also make no room for grace. Self-aware people see their sin. A perfectionist either rejects grace or denies imperfection, both which act as ankle bracelets that track us to unreachable standards.

Let grace choke out your perfectionism. Don't accept sloppiness or anything less than excellence, but realize that excellence is the combination of diligence, learning, and hustle. Perfection is not a part of excellence, and it actually hinders your performance.

Embracing the grace of Christ is not merely a tactic to help you improve your performance at work. No, embracing the grace offered by Jesus is *salvation*. We had better come to the throne of grace looking for eternal salvation—a place to rest our soul—before we try this business of letting grace kill our perfectionism. Salvation in Jesus is a simple matter, but it is all that matters. Once saved, once bathed in the blood of Jesus, we can then rise from the tomb of our old selves and walk in the new day of grace-filled living.

TAKE ACTION

Reflection: In what ways have you trusted in the lie that you can achieve perfection in your work? How might killing perfectionism free you to do great work? Write this down.

Prayer: The grace of Christ kills the need for perfectionism. Ask God to replace your desire to perform perfectly with a desire to live a life fully dependent upon Him. Write down your prayer.

<u>Action</u>: Walk outside. Look up at the sky and look down at the ground beneath your feet. Feel the air enter your lungs. You know who made all of that? God did. Do you know who sustains all of that? God does. Now, go on a short walk and think about the grace given in Christ. Let your perfectionism slip through your fingers.

Chapter 8

LEAD BY SERVING

Different thinking leads to different living—and, yes, different working. Now that we have addressed some of the walls that stand between our faith and our work, let's roll up our sleeves and look forward. What can we do differently today to work more faithfully? We'll start with the hugely important concept of leadership.

Lieutenant Michael Murphy was pinned down. Murphy, a Navy SEAL, was the leader of a four-man reconnaissance unit in the Hindu Kush Mountains of Afghanistan. And his team was in big trouble. Greatly outnumbered by enemy fighters, Murphy and his team fought like lions to keep the enemy at bay. As they shot, moved, and hunkered down behind jagged boulders, they killed many adversaries, but the mountain seemed to spawn more men with AK-47s who sprayed lead in their direction. Debris and bullets snapped all around them. They ran low on ammo.

They were overrun.

Murphy and his team were shot up, blown up, and exhausted—but still alive. So they fought hard. Murphy was the radio guy, and he was responsible to communicate with the base. If they were going to get help, Murphy needed to do something immediately. He did. Murphy ran to an open spot where he could get reception—exposed to enemy fire—and called out over the airwaves for air support. He knew exactly what he was doing—what the stakes were for being out in the open. The mountain opened up on Murphy in that moment, and a bullet tore through his back. He completed the call and fought for as long as he was conscious, but he died soon thereafter.

This is the essence of leadership. In the face of death, Murphy served his men. He took a hail of bullets to serve his squad on that mountain. Murphy served to death. (One man made it out alive, Marcus Luttrell, and he wrote a book memorializing the event called *Lone Survivor*.)

Great leaders know that they are servants, not kings. A leader is blessed not because he has hordes of minions, but because there are a bunch of people whom he can serve. And this is a great responsibility, to have many under your care. A leader of many can serve many, and a leader of few can serve few—but both are both blessed to serve.

When Jesus said it is better to give than to receive, He was not speaking in a parable. Though Jesus loved to answer questions with questions and infuse His teaching with mystery, His admonition to choose a service-minded approach was clear. Straight up, it is better for us to give than to receive—to serve rather than be served. Not only is it better for those we serve, but it's also better for us to serve other people. Our best interest is tied to the best interest of others, and through serving we obtain the deep-seated joy of sharing the love of Christ with someone else. There's something in it for us when we serve.

In economics, one of the fundamental principles underlying all theories is that people act in their own best interest. This is an assumption that economists make, a truth underlying the rest of their findings. That is how capitalism works. You may hear this and scoff. Those greed-mongering bad guys with their white collars and big bonuses! Those self-interested crooks!

I am talking about you.

We all act in our own self-interest, whether we admit it or not. If you boil down your motivation for something, you will find that there was something in it for you. And allow me to let you in on a secret: this is okay. It is even good. God did not design the world such that we should ignore our interest.

C.S. Lewis says it brilliantly in *The Weight of Glory*:

If you asked twenty good men today what they thought the highest of the virtues, nineteen of them would reply, Unselfishness. But if you had asked almost any of the great Christians of old, he would have replied, Love. You see what has happened? A negative term has been substituted for a positive, and this is of more than philological importance. The negative idea of Unselfishness carries with it the suggestion not primarily of securing good things for others, but of going without them ourselves, as if our abstinence and not their happiness was the important point. I do not think this is the Christian virtue of Love. The New Testament has lots to say about self-denial, but not about self-denial as an end in itself.[9]

Love is a higher virtue than self-denial. The point is to "[secure] good things for others," not deprive ourselves. But these two concepts must marry together. Love requires self-denial at times, but that self-denial is a means to love. Do you see the difference?

Love that costs something means something. That is why Jesus' death on the cross has changed the history of the world. It cost everything, and my God does it ever mean something.

Bundle love and self-denial together, and God provides the rest. Our self-interest is handled by our sovereign Father. If God does not exist, we had better get ours. It's up to us to procure stuff of value and pile it up so we can climb on top and descend toward the ground in depression as it rots beneath us. But if He does exist, God is involved, and He cares about our well-being. He knows when a bird falls and He knows the number of hairs on our head. God won't overlook our desires—He will fulfill them. It just won't be how we planned.

Servant Leadership

> *It shall not be so among you. But whoever would be great among you must be your servant, and whoever would be first among you must be your slave, even as the Son of Man came not to be served but to serve, and to give his life as a ransom for many.*
>
> —Matthew 20:26-28

James and John were all in. They knew Jesus and wanted to be closer to Him. As we catch up with them in the above verse in Matthew, they are hanging out with Jesus in the flesh. Then, as well-meaning moms are wont to do, their mom showed up to embarrass them. She came up to Jesus and asked if, well, ya know, maybe they could get the seats next to Jesus in heaven.

Jesus tells her she doesn't know what she's asking. If James and John are looking for position, they are going about it the wrong way. I guess it didn't hurt to ask, but the question revealed a deep misunderstanding of the way the world works. You see, Jesus knew He must soon drink the cup of the wrath of God, a deadly beverage which turns the skies black.

He turns to James and John: "Are you able to drink the cup that I am to drink?"

Can you imagine what was going through their mind at this point?

Jesus then tells them that they will indeed share His cup (though surely they had no idea what that entailed) but that the Father will dictate who sits where. Jesus' point: serve, and God will handle the rest. We don't have to obsess over our position if we will serve boldly. James and John could never drink the cup Jesus was to drink. They weren't even worthy to do so.

The rest of the disciples heard this conversation. And they were not happy about their boys James and John jockeying for position. (Probably because they themselves wanted the good seats next to Jesus.) Jesus sees this as a perfect opportunity to teach them about *servant leadership*.

Jesus turns to the group and explains that leaders must serve and give their lives over for the good of those under their care. He even uses the word *slave*. Leaders must put themselves last, but more importantly, they must put others first. A leader must even operate as a slave, serving with great cost.

You are a leader. The concept of servant leadership applies to you, regardless of your position at work. You lead someone, somewhere. It may be your kids or it may be a friend or it may be a Fortune 500 company, but someone looks to you for guidance. And you must understand the importance of your influence.

When you think of a leader, you might picture the president of the U.S. with teams of slick-suited Secret Service agents inconspicuously placed to protect them. Or maybe you picture the CEO of a publicly-traded company with a huge office and a jet. Maybe you picture a general in the field with his men. Sure, these guys are leaders—but don't relegate the concept of leadership to other people. You will forget your own duty.

Be ready to serve in leadership. Look around you to see those for whom you are responsible—professionally or otherwise—and seek to learn how you can improve their situation, or how you can encourage them. This is not to say that a leader needs to throw out their calendar and disregard time management to walk around giving out cups of water at the office because someone just might be thirsty. No, a leader must invest their efforts in their area of maximum effectiveness for the mission of the organization—and that mission had better mean something.

A servant leader is an effective leader. Serving builds relationships and engenders trust, and trust greases the gears of a company. Low trust rusts the gears and slows everything down.

One of the leaders I respect most is Dave Ramsey. I have had the honor of briefly meeting him and some of his leaders at the Ramsey Solutions headquarters in Nashville, Tennessee. Walking into the Ramsey Solutions headquarters is like walking into your living room. You are served from the moment you walk into the door. To the left as you walk in, there is a welcoming cafe and a friendly face offering freshly-baked cookies, coffee, and water. A guest at Ramsey Solutions is treated like a guest in a home. But it doesn't stop there.

The reason I went to the Ramsey Solutions headquarters was to interview Ken Coleman, the host of the EntreLeadership podcast. (Ken is also the author of *One Question*, which is a book I highly recommend you pick up.) Let me be straight here: I had no business interviewing Ken Coleman or anyone else for that matter. I was traveling with my buddy Brad. We were just regular dudes with no fame or following, but for some reason Ken agreed to do the interview. Brad was there to film the interview, and I was there to ask the questions. What Ken didn't know is that I had never interviewed someone on camera before. Brad and I were in over our heads.

But as we met Ken and the producer of the podcast, Eric, we were immediately put at ease. These guys wanted to make sure we were comfortable. They were gracious hosts to a couple of nobodies. And they treated each other the same way, with warmth and deference and respect. Servant leadership walks the halls of Ramsey Solutions.

Selling great software serves people. Fixing a transmission serves people. The concept of servant leadership—of putting yourself in the position of a servant rather than a king—is applicable to all work situations.

And God will tell you where to sit.

Make People Cry

A close friend of mine once worked at one of those big toxic companies that people love to hate. Okay, it was an airline. The reason you may loathe to fly on this company's planes is that the culture at the gate and inside the plane is just an extension of the culture of the company itself, or so I learned.

Anyway, my friend held a position in finance and strategy. I was appalled when he told me how their meetings went. Everyone would give their report on their sector while their bosses would fire questions and criticism faster than they could answer. It was like a gauntlet of irresponsible leadership where the goal was to question the legitimacy of everyone's efforts.

Like I said, the environment was toxic.

One time, my friend was walking the halls of this dark company, and he saw a guy in his cube. He looked sad. So my friend asked him how he was doing. And as the downtrodden cube-dweller explained what was going on, he began to cry. He was overwhelmed that my friend had cared enough to stop and check on him. "No one has ever done that before," he said with a cracked voice.

I had an experience with a large company that still blows my mind. My company was a vendor to theirs. This company treats people like units or tools or machines—anything but humans. Well, this one person was treating me and my team horrifically. Demanding calls at all hours on my phone, and if you didn't answer, she'd call again and email and call until you did. Everything this person said was something we "needed" to do, and she monopolized everyone's time.

I had enough. I called her to talk things over and explained that we need to establish some boundaries of respect. I explained this behavior slowed my company down and made it harder to fix problems. The conversation didn't go well, and I thought my company might get fired. We were in the middle of a project and getting canned would cost lots of money—and their lawyers were bigger than our lawyers.

Rough though it was, after the call we did establish a new level of respect. I began to see behind the curtain that the pressure at this company started inside its walls and extended outward to vendors. Domineering leadership in, domineering leadership out. A culture of bad leadership breeds bad leaders. And it pervades every level of the organization.

It is never "just business." That saying makes me cringe, as it is usually said in the context of one person trampling on another for gain. People are valuable children of God. When we gaze upon the glint of God's image in our fellow man, it makes it a little harder to treat them like livestock. Good leaders respect other people, but great leaders love. And love costs something and rearranges your Wednesday afternoon without notice. If you care about your people enough to love them—not because they are lovable (like you, sometimes they aren't) but because they are objects of God's love—you will lead them well.

Leadership is tough, though. Love doesn't mean pizza parties and bean bag chairs all day. There is work to be done. And as a leader you will make hard choices for the good of the whole. For example, sometimes the most loving thing you can do is to fire a person. A staff member who does not work hard costs everyone else on the team. Grow your team members, hold them accountable, give them a chance—but if a person is not shaping up, you will have to do what you have to do eventually. Enabling is just harm shrouded in passivity. It is best to be clear and cut to the chase. A firefighter friend of mine calls this "strong love."

We are compelled by the gospel to love deeply in all situations. Our leadership should have a warmth that encourages, uplifts, and soothes—and that just might make someone cry.

Curious and Humble Management

I remember in my early twenties I had it all figured out. I think that's a pretty normal delusion to have when you're in your early twenties. The business world should work like this and our company should do this and that. I knew where all of the pieces fit.

Except that I didn't.

I should have asked some questions and asked someone who actually knew what they were talking about. You know, someone who had traveled the road I was on. Thankfully my youthful naivety didn't cost me much, and even if it did, the lesson was worth the cost. I learned to learn.

I have heard it said that the time gap between stimulus and response is the measure of maturity. For example, when you get a contentious email, how long do you sit on your response? How much do you pray, think, and wait so your response will be thoughtful and balanced? I don't know about you, but I tend to just knee-jerk respond. But some time and observation would be helpful.

Leaders must approach situations with the eyes of an eager student. Scripture says we need to be quick to hear and slow to speak.

> *Know this, my beloved brothers: let every person be quick to hear, slow to speak, slow to anger.*
> *—James 1:19*

I figure that the reason we have two ears and one mouth is because we ought to listen twice as much as we talk. This is true in all spheres of life, but it's certainly true at work. The right question brings clarity and lights up the room. An attuned ear finds opportunity, while a reckless mouth creates problems.

When we listen first, we put ourselves in a position to care—to empathize. And when we are curious and humble as leaders of others, we just might learn something important. We cannot be at all places at all times, nor can we be infinitely wise. But we can build a relationship with our team such that we are a safe place to bring information. We can show respect and lend an ear.

Listen, learn, and observe. Don't assume you know.

A servant leader is an effective leader. It takes courage to lead with love and to take a personal interest in those around you. It may look weird and unusual, and in such case you're probably on the right track. The default mode of leadership is to grab power, hold on tight, and show everyone how powerful you are. Servant leadership is just the opposite—to show people how powerful they are. Illuminating the potential of your team versus highlighting your own greatness is not only right, it is effective.

Leaders are the drivers of our world. And God directs the path of leaders as He wishes (Proverbs 21:1). We need more godly leaders, men and women who get stuff done for the good of their team. People who understand we aren't a bunch of robots and that our mission goes beyond mere commerce.

God has placed you in a unique position. He has given you a life to lead and has given you people to lead. The people around you need you to lead by serving, to show them your strength by leveraging your might for their benefit. Leaders serve and servants lead—if Jesus' example is any indication.

Serve, lead, and keep learning.

TAKE ACTION

Reflection: Who do you lead? Your family? Those who work for you? Your friends? Consider (and write down) all of the people with whom you have influence.

Prayer: Jesus is the ultimate servant leader. He led in the purest form and He served by paying the ultimate price on the cross. Pray to Jesus and thank Him for His act of service on the cross for you. Ask Jesus how you might better serve others. Write down your prayer.

Action: Perform one act of service today for someone you lead. For example, if you have a team of three underneath you, try taking one of them aside to ask how you can help them be more successful, or just take them to lunch. Also, pray for those who you lead and write down your prayer for them.

Chapter 9

MAKE TENTS

After this Paul left Athens and went to Corinth. And he found a Jew named Aquila, a native of Pontus, recently come from Italy with his wife Priscilla, because Claudius had commanded all the Jews to leave Rome. And he went to see them, and because he was of the same trade he stayed with them and worked, for they were tentmakers by trade. And he reasoned in the synagogue every Sabbath, and tried to persuade Jews and Greeks.

—*Acts 18:1-4*

Having established that we want to lead by serving—as Jesus did—we now approach the elephant in the room for us laypersons (those of us who are not vocational ministers). We have a day job, some might say a "secular" job, so we need to understand how our work outside the church affects the church and connects to our community.

The apostle Paul wasn't just a preacher and an evangelist—he made tents. He was a bi-vocational guy, meaning he had two jobs. Paul worked his day job making tents so he could do ministry. The tent-making gig was the only one that paid. So the most famous preacher in history—I mean, come on, the guy wrote a ton of the Bible—was a blue-collar working man. Paul was a regular guy who worked and sweated and loved Jesus so much he couldn't help but tell others the Good News.

So often we think we "can't do something like *that*" or that our responsibilities are too heavy for us to pursue bold and meaningful work. We think that our day jobs make us so busy, we're all so busy, *I mean have you seen how busy I am*? We think our lives are maxed out when they are really just disorganized and not properly focused.

Further, we deceive ourselves if we believe that there's sacred work and there's secular work and the two are mutually exclusive. Work is work, and while the call to preach the Gospel from the pulpit is indeed a noble calling, we are all called to preach the gospel with our lives—and with our work.

Paul's lifestyle wasn't something he came up with on a couch with his therapist. He didn't read some ministry strategy book or go to a tent-making conference; he just made tents because it paid the bills, and he preached because he couldn't help it. Pretty simple.

Paul met Jesus on a dirt road. That day, his old self died. He was blind for three days until he opened his eyes again to see the light of the world in light of Jesus. Old Paul—persecutor of Christians. New Paul—evangelistic maniac. Jesus changed his name from Saul to Paul to show a new man was born.

But was the only reason Paul made tents to fund his ministry? He had lots of costs to cover with travel and food and lodging—and he clearly hated depending on others financially. So yeah, he needed to work to bring in money, but was that the sole purpose of his tent business?

I don't think so.

Paul was a holistic thinker. He didn't compartmentalize well. And he thought practically. There were no neat little boxes for Paul's faith and work. Paul followed Jesus everywhere he went.

To separate Paul's faith from his work, you'd have to rip out Paul's beating heart. In fact, I'd imagine Paul was tough to be around sometimes. You might just want to grab a glass of wine with him, and he'd probably lay some stinging truth on the table.

Paul's friend: "This is some good wine. I get notes of coriander and honey."

Paul: "You are going to die very soon. Are you making the best use of your time?"

Paul's friend: "Uhh . . ."

Paul saw no sacred/secular divide. Paul didn't see a wall between his faith and the rest of his life *because his faith was his life*. It would be like removing the water from the ocean—no water, no ocean. No Jesus, no Paul. Just Saul, the persecutor of Christians. A different dude entirely.

So Paul made tents as an important part of his ministry. Tents did fund his preaching, but making tents provided a valuable opportunity to serve and love and share the Good News. I picture Paul sitting cross-legged with needles and thread and tent canvas on the dirt floor of a house. As he worked quietly with Aquila on a tent, Paul shared stories from the road and encouraged Aquila in his faith. Making tents carved out ministry opportunities for Paul.

Over the years I have had several people ask me if I intended to go into the vocational ministry. I'm not sure why. The answer to that question is that yes, though I am a layman in the business world, I *am* in the vocational ministry. And so are you. Our jobs are ministry.

If our jobs are ministry—and they are—let's get practical. How do we integrate our faith into our work and turn our jobs into missions?

Tithe

The concept of giving to the church has been muddied and stained by sin and irresponsible church leadership. We've seen televangelists claim that if you just give to them they'll make you rich and healthy, then the news finds out they're liars (shocker). I have sat in the pews of a church as the lead pastor pressured us with a sermon and then, oh look there, there was a credit card slip in the back of the chair that he wanted everyone to turn in.

But we cannot let stupid human behavior denigrate a sacred blessing—and giving money to the local church is indeed a blessing. God doesn't need our money. He spoke us into being with words, no organic material needed. He doesn't go to Home Depot to stock up on DNA; He just speaks whatever He wishes into being. So He surely doesn't need 10 percent of your paycheck to handle His business. But the local church might.

The local church is the most sacred of entities, the bride of Christ. He purchased her with His blood on the cross. When we are saved, we are saved into a people—the church. And she—the church—takes money to run efficiently. I have been involved in pastoring a local church for numerous years now. I have seen the church grow from a dream (literally) to a thriving church family. So I have gotten to see how church finances work. Let me show you behind the curtain, especially if you're skeptical. Even though this is just one church, maybe this will help you see that good churches exist.

We are elder-led, meaning we have an elder board of pastors (lay and vocational) who all hold the same amount of decision-making power. No one is king. We are arranged in various sectors: missions, benevolence, preaching, etc. This helps to avoid any power mongering and brings fresh perspectives into the mix. As one of the elders, I have seen our church fight for frugality, effectiveness, and most importantly, an eternal rate of return (ERR) on its money (meaning we seek to maximize the gospel impact of every dollar). I've watched our underpaid lead pastor vie for less money so the church could have more money. I have seen single moms blessed by the local church, and I have seen other churches planted by our church. Maybe we're a unicorn, but I have never seen anything but a healthy perspective on stewardship, budgeting, and financial management. And that's all to God's credit, as He protects and cares for His church.

Here is my point: your tithe matters to the local church. Find a church that preaches the gospel and loves people, and commit totally (including your finances). As (hopefully) a member of a local church, it's your job to give. If you find a perversion of leadership or some major issue, address it. But Scripture calls us to give with a glad heart, not a skeptical heart.

Remember how Jesus said it's better to give than to receive? Money falls into that. Your tithe probably won't get you a big house with a dolphin fountain and a Ferrari in the driveway, but there is a joyful return on your giving that cannot rust or get repo'd. You cannot out-give God—He has already given that which we cannot repay in Christ. The joy just keeps on coming.

The local church is funded by regular Joes. People who work and tithe. Some have little and thus can give little, while others write six-figure checks, but it doesn't matter. God's beautiful design includes hard-working people toiling and giving a portion of their income to the sacred institution of the local church. If you aren't tithing, I encourage you to start immediately. Giving is a sacred habit. Start small if you must, but cultivate this habit.

Tie your work to your tithe. As you go about your daily work, let the joy of working for the church flood your heart.

Seek the Welfare of the City

Build houses and live in them; plant gardens and eat their produce. Take wives and have sons and daughters; take wives for your sons, and give your daughters in marriage, that they may bear sons and daughters; multiply there, and do not decrease. But seek the welfare of the city where I have sent you into exile, and pray to the LORD on its behalf, for in its welfare you will find your welfare.

—Jeremiah 29:5-7

Your work will change your city. The work of your hands—whatever that may be—changes the world one day at a time. You may wonder how your estate planning business or your landscaping company "changes the world." Well, it does. And it needs to.

First, the way in which you work influences others. If you come to work as Eeyore every day, lamenting your job and your boss and *is it Friday yet*, you'll spread your negativity to others. They will see you, and if they know about your faith in Christ, they will wonder what's up. *If this guy claims to be full of hope and passion, why does he whine and never get any work done?* But if you go to work with your mind right, you'll bring honor and glory to Christ. Others, both believers and non-believers, will want to know more about what makes you tick. We don't use the word *honor* much anymore, as irreverence is more popular, but when you operate with a sense of honor, your colleagues and clients will take notice. And they just might follow your lead as you walk behind Jesus.

Second, your work produces something. Again, it could be great estate plans or it could be beautiful lawns—but your work shapes the world. So you might want to pay attention to what mark you're leaving. Jesus was a carpenter before He started His ministry at the age of 30, and this was no accident. Carpentry is a rough and ordinary business, not glamorous or lucrative. Jesus was strategic, and He had a tremendous amount of work to accomplish before He met His destiny on Calvary—so He didn't waste any of His life. As He built things from wood, He beautified Nazareth and He blessed His customers. He turned God's raw organic material into something with useful form. Each project changed the way the world looked, one at a time.

Our welfare—our well-being—is tied to that of our city. When we seek to care for our neighbors and our city, we seek to care for ourselves. Remember how economists build economic models based upon the assumption that all people seek their self-interest?

Philippians 2:4 says that we should look not only to our own interests, but also to the interests of others. Paul worked hard making tents so he could eat and wear clothes—he looked out for himself. You want to be happy and to have a job you love. You want to lead a joy-filled life. Me too. Lean into that, understanding that your joy is a good thing and your well-being is important.

Here is the deal—I cannot feed you if I am starving to death myself. I cannot love you if I have no love in my heart. I cannot give you a place to rest if I have no home. We must care for ourselves such that we are strong, capable instruments in God's hands. And then we can look to the interests of others as our primary mission, because that's where our well-being lies. Theirs too.

Your work should solve two problems: 1) your needs and 2) the needs of others. If you have one or the other, you are out of whack. Focus on number 1 and you'll be a greed monger, and focus on number 2 and you'll grow weary and lose effectiveness to continue. Our towns and cities need us to work hard, to produce valuable goods and services. Our neighbors need us to look to their interests.

Dedicate your work to the welfare of your city.

Flip Your Thinking (You *Get* to Work)

This whole Monday to Friday thing has to stop. Those of us in America live in lavish times. Our poor are considered rich in other parts of the world. I don't intend to demean the real struggles of some, the hungry kids and the homeless wanderers, but if you're reading this book you are better off than most of the world—and you probably have your needs met. In the Maslow's hierarchy of needs, you've reached the self-actualization stage. If you're burning this book for warmth in a trash barrel, maybe not.

Healthcare is expensive, and the tax man taketh, and all that.

Sure. But the standard of living with which we have become accustomed is far beyond what we need to survive. So we should first be thankful to God for keeping His promise to provide. In the numbness of comfort, we often forget the abundance in which we live. We need to flip our thinking about work.

"I *have* to work this weekend."

"I can't man, I *have* to work."

"What time do you *have* to be at work?"

No, we *get* to work. According the Bureau of Labor Statistics, the national unemployment rate at the time of this writing is right at 5 percent for folks over 16 years old.[10] That means 95 percent of people who want work have jobs. What this means is if you hustle, think creatively, and are willing to do hard and messy work, you will find a job. You have that choice.

So you choose to work. Why? Because you want to eat and because stuff costs money and maybe people are depending on you. But you choose to work—and you choose *where* you work. In a free country, no one held a pistol to your back and brought you to your job interview. Your résumé wasn't written by the Ministry of Labor and then forced into the hands of your employer who then forcibly hired you. This was a choice you made.

Now, maybe you made a bad choice. I've been there. Sometimes in our fallibility we make stupid moves and our life suffers. But there's only us to blame.

We have already established that God created work as a blessing. In fact, it was our first blessing. We don't lament when we enjoy other blessings from God. Why then do we begrudge work?

It's all about mindset.

If you understand that work is a blessing, you will believe that you *get* to work. If you believe that work is a curse, you will *have* to work. If you believe the Bible is the inerrant word of God, you agree that you *get* to work. It does not mean that work does not contain thorns and thistles or that sweat won't drip off your brow as you toil to make ends meet, but it means that while work is cursed it isn't itself a curse. See the difference? I cannot imagine that Jesus ever whined about carpentry. He may have smashed His thumb or got a gnarly splinter or dropped a beam on His head, but Jesus could not have lamented His work given His perfect character. As our example, He would have dishonored the Father who sent Him by dishonoring the work He was sent to do. Jesus understood that He was blessed to work, sweat and splinters and slow times and all.

Assess yourself. Do you believe that you *have* to work or that you *get* to work? Does it scare you to think that we will work in heaven or that God's first blessing to us humans was to get to work? Be honest—it's okay.

We are ill-deserving of the grace of Christ. We deserve judgment, but the Father rendered His Son to die for us instead. So too are we ill-deserving of the lavish common graces He sends our way: work, the sun, air in our lungs, life today. Ill-deserving people ought to maintain a posture of thankfulness, not because they ought to, but because they understand their blessed condition.

Most of us are not vocational ministers, but we are in vocational ministry. Your job is a ministry, and you have a mission to accomplish: to honor God in your work and to seek the interests of others. The sacred/secular divide is man-made, and it is a wall that we must walk through. The saints fill the pews, but they also fill the cubes.

You might struggle with connecting your lay job to divine ministry, but that is probably due to wrong thinking conditioned by the entitled culture in which you live. As you check your heart, and most importantly seek Scripture and prayer, your lenses will change. You see, Jesus makes new men and women when they meet Him. Their name and rank and job changes. Paul is not Saul. And if you know Jesus, though you may not be a super-sanctified hero Christian, you are certainly not who you used to be.

From what I have seen, our jobs lag behind in our sanctification. We rightly want to kill the porn habit or the binge drinking, but what about our laziness at the office? Or said more positively, we say we want to love our neighbors and to serve our fellow man—but what about the opportunity to love and serve your boss? You've got about eight hours a day of opportunity there.

Our life contains no compartments—it's just life. Now there are sectors of life: work, family, recreation, etc., but we are the same person walking through each. Or we should be. Jesus says that whoever seeks to keep his life will lose it, but whoever loses his life will find it (Luke 17:33). If we embrace the power of the gospel at work, we'll find that our tent-making becomes gloriously purposeful. And purpose brings joy.

TAKE ACTION

Reflection: In what ways (big or small) might your work bless your city? Consider the benefits of your job and consider how your contribution shows your community the love of God. Write down these benefits/blessings of your work.

Prayer: Our work needs to be yoked to a big purpose. Working only for a paycheck is empty and misses the point. Ask God how you can bless others in your work, both inside and outside of your immediate circle of influence. Write this down.

Action: The next time you are paid, take a portion of your check and give it away. If you aren't already tithing, give the money to the local church. If you are tithing, consider what a one-time gift could mean for your church or someone in need. The size of your gift can be big or small—that's up to you. Write down and consider the blessed opportunity to have the resources to give money away because of God's gift of work.

_____

Chapter 10

WATCH THE CLOCK

Look carefully then how you walk, not as unwise but as wise, making the best use of the time, because the days are evil.

—Ephesians 5:15-16

We have tackled the five crucial walls (right thinking on money, assumptions, entitlement, culture, and perfectionism), and we have explored the idea of servant leadership. We now understand that we are all tent-makers and that our work is linked to the welfare of our community and our local church. Now we have today, right now. Let's explore how to make the best use of the gift of our time.

I respect Charles Spurgeon's writings and sermons. The guy had a wit coupled with zeal that is hard to find. He was a saintly maniac. He answered letters with his own pen, often working 18-hour days to get in all of his writing, sermon prep, and pastoral duties. I picture Spurgeon slumped over his desk, papers and spent cigars strewn everywhere as his stinging eyes search for something in a letter. 18 hours a day is a long time to work.

He died at age 57, having accomplished more for the cause of Christ than 20 regular men. He lived his life hard, filling every blank space with God's work. Spurgeon knew what he was doing with his time too. There were tradeoffs. You cannot work like that without your health and your family suffering to some degree. But he did a cost-benefit analysis each day and got up and did it again. He was a man obsessed with his mission, and his mission was to introduce people to Jesus and to pastor their souls.

Your work is a huge chunk of your life. Much of your time—for some people, most of their time—is spent working. So we absolutely must make sure we use this time wisely.

Time is like a river, it flows. Gently, constantly, one moment at a time, our life ticks by. You can sit still and try to slow down your observation of time (meditation, solitude) or you can run around like a headless chicken—but time neither waits nor speeds up for any man. We can only affect how we interact with how God doles out the increments of our life.

Carpe diem means to "seize the day." Seize it we must, squeezing out every drop for worthwhile purposes. We must not just seize our Saturdays; we must seize our Mondays. If you live to be 70, you'll have 3,650 of them.

Let's explore.

Efficiency = Effectiveness

If you want to be effective, to make things happen, you need to first manage your time. We can't focus on effectiveness first—that's the tail wagging the dog. Time-management precedes effectiveness. Legendary management consulting guru Peter Drucker urged his students to write down where their time goes before they could make any improvements in efficiency.

My version of trying to be efficient gets me walking too fast, talking too fast, and doing everything too fast. My dad and I are similar in that way. If you call me in the middle of a meeting, I might have business voice instead of my true voice and I might hurry off the phone. If I have lunch with you I'll fight the urge to check my email, and sometimes I might. So I'll start with a confession: I have an efficiency disorder. It throws me into frenzies. I hate wasting time during business hours, and I constantly feel guilty at the end of the day, convinced I could have seized more of the day.

If you're like me (Type A and focused), the clock will chase you around like an ankle-biting Chihuahua. You will never appease it until you train it—sort of. Our lives are set in a dichotomy of time. We control how we spend our time, but we can do nothing to control our time. Time management isn't really managing time—it's managing how we swim in the river of time. Like our money, time is a gift granted from God. We don't own it and we didn't create it, but we are called to steward it in our lives.

The first thing we need to do is to remove guilt from time management. If you are a Type A get-it-done type, you will especially be prone to setting standards so high that four of you couldn't finish your to-do list. If you are continuously guilty at the end of the day like I am, you probably need to take this medicine: *work hard, work smart, then get over yourself.* That felt good, right?

One more time: *work hard, work smart, then get over yourself.*

Maybe you think I'm weird for feeling guilty for not accomplishing enough. That's okay. In such case, you're probably a different breed than me but you still need the mantra of *work hard, work smart, then get over yourself.* You probably need more of the hard work component if you're always content with the effort you put out.

Let's explore each of these aspects:

1. <u>Work hard</u>. Self-explanatory, I hope. Put in the physical effort. Don't loaf on company time. Anything worth doing is worth doing well, as Dad always said. That sweat on your brow is good.

2. <u>Work smart</u>. Keep a calendar. Organize your time. Focus on the most important tasks, not the noisiest ones.

3. <u>Get over yourself</u>. You are not Jesus. You are not Superman. If you think that the world was short-changed by what you didn't get to, you're grossly overstating your importance to the world. God uses human instruments, but He isn't beholden to them.

Efficiency means moving forward diligently without being a busybody. Paul talks about busybodies in his letters. Paul intends to point out the difference between real hard work and lots of empty talk and frivolous activity. You know people like this. You may be a busybody yourself, always buzzing with action without anything getting done. If so, you can change this about yourself.

Okay, so we need to maximize our time and efficiency. Great. Maybe we should systematize our social life and our spiritual life, implementing a rigid schedule and a bunch of rules to make sure we are doing it right.

Or we could be warm-blooded human beings.

You are an instrument of God's work, yes. You have some big things to do in your life, and it is important that you manage the allotment of time you've been given. But you are not a robot. An instrument, not a robot. A violin, not a crescent wrench (well, sometimes a crescent wrench). Efficiency is respecting the scarcity of time and hustling while trusting God to provide the increase.

Every year around New Year's Eve, I sit down to write my goals. I usually sit on my back porch with a good cigar and something to drink. I have my Bible and my journal, and I think about the past year. I start writing goals. In the previous five years, I've categorized my goals into spiritual, family, business, personal, and health. Each goal has bullet points of a goal, and the goal must be specific and measurable. At the end of this session, when the cigar is all ashes, it's time to get up and do something else.

It's a nice little ritual, except for one problem: I never do anything with these goals. Now maybe it's just a good excuse to hang out on the back porch, but I do think this goal-setting session has value. It's just that life is a smeared abstract canvas, not a graduate school thesis. Goals matter. Really they do. But I start to think that my goals reign supreme and that I had better be efficient and effective to execute those goals. If not life is wasted, I'm chasing a windy idol.

James 4 says it better:

> Come now, you who say, "Today or tomorrow we will go into such and such a town and spend a year there and trade and make a profit"—yet you do not know what tomorrow will bring. What is your life? For you are a mist that appears for a little time and then vanishes. Instead you ought to say, "If the Lord wills, we will live and do this or that." As it is, you boast in your arrogance. All such boasting is evil. So whoever knows the right thing to do and fails to do it, for him it is sin.
>
> —James 4:13-17

An atheist's goals are supremely valuable. It is his meaning in life. Even if he only sets the goal of having the most fun possible, his meaning is found in accomplishing exactly what he wants out of this short mist of a life. He is both god and beneficiary. A Christian, on the other hand, should set goals based upon an intention to align his will with God's will. Goals are set with submission as a caveat—"I'll do this and that, God willing."

Slam on the gas, and get to work. God is sovereign and He will do what He wants with you.

Efficiency is maximizing time. Effectiveness is getting things done. Work hard on the right tasks and you'll find both. But remember that your degree of effectiveness is not yours to decide. God will need to bring rain, sun, and warmth on your efforts for you to be maximally effective.

Do your part. He'll do His.

Rectangular Black Holes

Stephen King calls the television the glass teat. We sit in front of the glowing box with a bunch of images and sounds thrown together and just take it all in. Imagine if you will that the sounds and images have a visible stream flowing into your brain. It's like a flooded river, light brown and strewn with debris, raging into unknown places. We take in a lot of stimuli that the brain absorbs. Those images and sounds stay within us in our subconscious, each one a deposit into our mental account.

How about your phone? Tim Ferriss calls that one the cocaine pellet dispenser. We, the apex of the food chain, hunch over this tiny little screen looking for affirmation or promotion or entertainment or escape. I know I have been in checkout lines immersed in my cocaine pellet dispenser and hardly knew where I was. Years ago I remember sitting in the food court of an airport between flights. I had my journal and my Bible and C.S. Lewis's *The Weight of Glory*, so I had high hopes for my time at this cheap metal table. I read some and wrote some, but then I was distracted, disturbed even, when I realized that everyone was looking at a phone. Like everyone. The guy in the suit. The mom in security dragging her messy-haired toddler in pajamas. The rangy-looking fellow who is either a musician or a terrorist. They were all on their phones, rectangular handheld portals to somewhere else. They weren't mentally at the airport.

The television streams information to us. We are on the

receiving end of the information flow, and it comes hard and fast—and forever if we let it. Our phones are the opposite; we scroll and refresh and search for something in there: that email, that affirming like, that post, that article. One brings stuff to us, and the other we pour ourselves into, looking for something. The result is the same: distraction from the real, non-pixelated world around us.

What are we doing? Have you ever thought about that?

Our world now allows zero boredom. Boredom has been killed. If you are bored you probably want to be. Lines no longer allow conversation with a stranger. Waiting in the doctor's office is a chance to crack out on our phones instead of meeting a stranger. Evenings are opportunities robbed by glowing boxes, glass teats, cocaine pellet dispensers.

History has no precedent for this new frontier. We have no idea where this is going. I have heard people say that technology is moving forward so quickly that artificially intelligent robots are going to take over the world like in *Terminator*. Those are the same people who have alien stickers on their cars and are getting ready for the zombie apocalypse, so maybe we should take what they say with a grain of salt. But seriously, we don't know where technology will take the human race.

Here's the deal: we become what we behold. If we behold random flickering pixels all day long, I guess we'll become flickering people. On. Off. There. Here. Nowhere. I'd rather behold Jesus, but I just "be holding" my phone.

Go ahead. Tell me about your Bible apps and your daily devotional. You stay connected with old friends, right? You've got all of this under control.

I don't.

This technology addiction is crazy, and I don't know where it's going. I'll take a step back from my desk to scroll through feeds because I am tied to this magic machine. I cannot imagine what this is doing to my brain, my switching on and off. Oh— you're above that? Now you're a liar *and* an addict.

I can tell you what it's doing to my work: it's destroying it and making it smaller.

If you were to sort through your interactions with screens yesterday, what would you find? Place the stuff that makes you mad over there, the nonsense over there, the dog pictures here . . . now what if you created a pie chart to look at the proportions of things. How big would your category be for things that added eternal value to your life—screen interactions that brought love, peace, fun, and Jesus to your life? For me, that category is just about empty most days.

I'm a bit of a laggard when it comes to technology. I got involved in social media when I started writing this book. The experts say you can't just write a book and set it on your front porch for people—you have to promote it with what the writing industry calls a platform. I read books about building a platform and how to act in social media settings (fork on the right or left?). I gave it a shot. But then I got sucked into the vortex. *How many likes? How many shares? Does anyone care?* As an old soul (I'm 32 going on 72), I walked out of 1920 into the new world to try to build a platform to sell books, but I felt like a caveman walking into a movie theater. (I'm still there, by the way.)

I missed the point.

We are social creatures. God made us communal. And that's why we seek all of this glowing pixel time. Something about it makes us feel connected, affirmed—or at least we hope it will. The value is in the people on the other end of the glowing boxes or by the stories we are told.

Don't trash all of your technology; redeem it. Take it back. You and I are made to create stuff, not endlessly consume the stuff others have made. We must bring this mindset with us to our virtual lives, meaning we should seek to add value to the lives of others through our interactions. And they *are* virtual lives. You and I exist in the open air, in parks and houses and streets and cars. That social media profile—that isn't you. It is merely a representation of who you are from the right angle with the right light. So if you have a massive following on Twitter, don't think you're that special. If you have a handful of followers, don't think you're any less valuable or interesting. We have got to (I have got to) free ourselves from the psychological and spiritual prison of addiction to affirmation through a screen. It zaps our time and kills our effectiveness at work.

Drink it In

Go, eat your bread with joy, and drink your wine with a merry heart, for God has already approved what you do.
—Ecclesiastes 9:7

We are on a conveyor belt of death. Each moment's passing brings us closer to dying. We all know this, but we act as if we don't, searching unceasingly for stuff to fill the void of time instead of filling the void in our hearts. That's a sad state of living.

The colors of the world are always brightest right after a funeral. You mope to your car, lips sealed in reverence, and shut the door. The silence embraces you. If you're with someone, every word is blasphemy, even if you just need to stop at the 7-Eleven to use the restroom. We are 14 again, with every word spoken in hesitant embarrassment of knowing we probably should just be quiet.

Why? Why do funerals bring this cold molasses awkwardness? One word: *reverence.*

Funerals bring the unspeakable subject of death into plain view. We are there to mourn and celebrate someone who has died. And we must come to grips with our mortality. And no one likes to do that.

Have you ever thought about the fact that we are wireless

creatures? We aren't plugged into an energy source with a cord. Our hearts just thump, thump, thump, in a life-giving muscle contraction until someday it goes *thump—thu—t*. God is the energy source, of course. And He keeps us thump, thumping until our earthly expiration date.

Funerals deliver the sure knowledge that our thumping will cease just like our beloved friend or relative. We are sad for them and scared for us. Even though those of us that follow Jesus know death is a doorway and not being blotted off the face of existence, death is a black void that none of us have experienced yet (unless you're one of those children who come on talk shows and talk about some there-and-back experience you had).

Each day—a Thursday or a Sunday—is a gift. And thus, hating your job is a real problem. We cannot spend our gifts in frustration looking for something else. If you've ever watched little kids open presents, you've seen this concept at work. They unwrap that pair of socks and then look around for something else because that gift isn't good enough. But hey—wait a minute—socks are pretty great, and they keep your feet warm. But little Sally doesn't care. What's next?

Some work days are like a pair of socks. Mundane but useful. Others are like a pair of socks with wasps in them. Others still like a pair of socks with 100-dollar bills stuffed inside.

But here is what I'd like for us to consider and explore: what does the normal day look like in your work? Not a horrible day and not a great day, just a *day*.

If the average work day for you is miserable, you need to do something about it. If you are so miserable that you complain and don't work hard, you need to do something about it yesterday. It could be that your job is not a fit for you, that your company is a toxic dump morally and spiritually, or that you are the problem. The latter is probably the issue.

A story is told that a newspaper once asked the English theologian G.K. Chesterton for a comment on the problem with the world (why all the pain, suffering, war, etc.). Chesterton allegedly replied,

Dear Sir:

I am.

Sincerely Yours,

G.K. Chesterton

If your work life is a daily dose of misery, you should start with yourself first. You are most likely the problem. And you can't fix you, try though you may. The gospel of Jesus Christ is that we cannot fix ourselves, but He can—and will. God helps those who *cannot* help themselves. So this self-assessment with your work is not a diagnostic test which will tell you exactly what you need to do with your work life, but rather a spiritual positioning exercise. (That sounds like an evening activity at a hippie commune, doesn't it? "The spiritual positioning exercise will begin after the yoga and self-centering session.") If you understand that you are probably the problem with your work, you can then proceed forward with doing something about your career with a clear head and a humble heart. But the first step is to repent and believe in the Gospel.

Suffering is an essential doctrine of the Christian life, but it must be suffering for the cause of Christ. Suffering because people hate the Jesus they see in us. God uses suffering as a paintbrush to make rainbows. But I don't think that you going to work every day in misery for forty years is what God has in mind. Useless suffering, or worse, self-inflicted suffering, is of no use.

We have to redeem our time, because we can't make more of it. We'll have to use it up, wear it out, make it do, or do without.

Joy and happiness are different. Joy is a permanent state of hopeful being, while happiness is a temporary state of emotional satisfaction. Joy lives in the heart of a man in all situations—

even the most horrific, while happiness flits this way and that and never stays around very long. Joy and happiness are linked, sure, but joy is better. And joy is the aim.

In Ecclesiastes, Solomon is not suggesting that we just drink wine and eat bread all the time and smile like fools. No, I believe his point is to use our time on this beautiful and broken earth wisely and to drink deeply of the joy of the Lord. Solomon had all of the riches in the world, and he learned that the real riches are in the belly of joy, not just cool stuff. And joy is found at the fountainhead—the feet of Jesus. So if we want our days to be joyful, we'll want to head to a deeper relationship with Jesus.

We spend a lot of our lifetime working. The clock ticks without our asking, and it will stop for no one. But God offers each day as a gift to enjoy and maximize. As Christians in the workplace, we should aim to redeem our time to make use of it and also to make joy of it. God unrolls each day before us clean and clear—and the day is ours to squander or use.

Our days are numbered on earth. Everyone breathes a first and last breath, the first choking and shocked, and the last much like the first. Scripture says that we are just a mist, here today and gone tomorrow. But we are headed somewhere, and this is just the first leg of the journey.

Take back your time and drink in every moment God gives you on this earth.

TAKE ACTION

Reflection: Where are you wasting your time (not enjoying rest, but wasting time)? Is technology a tool that helps you manage your time or does it take time away as it sucks you into its vortex? How might your investment of time shift to maximize your joy and your effectiveness? Write this down.

Prayer: God gives us our days. He makes the sun rise, and He holds the earth together. Ask God how you might enjoy Him more today. Write down several ways you can draw near to the Lord today (some hints: nature, Scripture, community, prayer).

Action: Act on the items written in the section above. Draw near to the Lord. Get up close to Him and trust His goodness and His mercy. Trust Him to inspire and empower the work of your hands.

CONCLUSION

The reason your work is so valuable is that you are infinitely valuable to God as His precious child. I wrote this book with the earnest hope that your mindset on work would shift to one of thankfulness, hard work, risk-taking, and creativity. In hopes that you'd never loathe another Monday and that you'd take ownership of this thing called work.

But that's just secondary.

My real hope is that through reading these pages and considering your work, you'd grow deeper in your relationship with Jesus, even if you presently have none. (If you made it to the conclusion of this book you are probably at least intrigued by the idea—so lean into that.) This whole job stuff doesn't mean much if your soul has no foundation and your heart has no delight. Nearness to Jesus is the aim.

You, my friend, are capable of doing more than you ever thought possible. God has great work for you to do on this earth, work so important that He prepared for you before time. Take no prisoners in your quest to integrate your faith and your work. And demolish those walls that get in the way.

NOTES

Chapter 1

1. Amy Adkins, "Majority of U.S. Employees Not Engaged Despite Gains in 2014," Gallup, January 28, 2015, accessed November 17, 2015, http://www.gallup.com/poll/181289/majority-employees-not-engaged-despite-gains-2014.aspx.

Chapter 2

2. John Piper, "Your Job as Ministry," June 14, 1981, accessed November 17, 2015, http://www.desiringgod.org/messages/your-job-as-ministry.

3. General George S. Patton, accessed November 17, 2015, http://www.generalpatton.com/quotes/.

Chapter 3

4. Cathleen Falsani, "The Worst Ideas of the Decade: The Prosperity Gospel," *The Washington Post*, accessed November 14, 2015, http://www.washingtonpost.com/wp-srv/special/opinions/outlook/worst-ideas/prosperity-gospel.html.

5. David Foster Wallace, *This Is Water: Some Thoughts, Delivered on a Significant Occasion, about Living a Compassionate Life* (New York: Little, Brown, & Company, 2009).

Chapter 6

6. Pew Research Center, "America's Changing Religious Landscape," May 12, 2015, accessed November 17, 2015, http://www.pewforum .org/2015/05/12/americas-changing-religious-landscape/.

7. Russell D. Moore, "Farewell, Cultural Christianity," July 1, 2015, accessed November 17, 2015, http://www.christianitytoday.com/ le/2015/july-web-exclusives/farewell-cultural-christianity.html.

8. Trevin Wax, "The Supreme Court Agrees with Hobby Lobby, but Your Neighbor Probably Doesn't," The Gospel Coalition, June 30, 2014, accessed November 17, 2015, http://blogs. thegospelcoalition.org/trevinwax/2014/06/30/the-supreme-court-agrees-with-hobby-lobby-but-your-neighbor-probably-doesnt/.

Chapter 8

9. C. S. Lewis, *The Weight of Glory* (New York: HarperOne, 1976), 24, https://books.google.com/books?id=WNTT_8NW_ qwC&printsec=frontcover&source=gbs_ge_summary_r&cad =0#v=onepage&q&f=false.

Chapter 9

10. Bureau of Labor Statistics, accessed November 17, 2015, http:// data.bls.gov/timeseries/LNS14000000.